THE
BOBBY McGREGOR
STORY

THE
BOBBY McGREGOR
STORY

BOBBY McGREGOR
& ATHOLE STILL

EYRE & SPOTTISWOODE
LONDON

First published 1970
© 1970 Bobby McGregor and Athole Still
Printed in Great Britain
for Eyre & Spottiswoode (Publishers) Ltd
11 New Fetter Lane, London E.C.4
by Latimer Trend & Co Ltd Plymouth

SBN 413 27680 5

Contents

5

Plates

7

Acknowledgement for permission to reproduce the plates is due
to the following: Keystone Press Agency Ltd for plates 1 and
16; Wheeler-Roberts Writers Ltd for plate 2a; Alex C. Cowper
for plate 3; Newspix, Blackpool for plate 4a; Bippa for plate 4b;
the *Scottish Daily Mail* for plate 5b; Central Press Photos Ltd
for plates 5c, 9a and 13b; and Sport and General Press Agency
for plates 9b and 13a.

All the diagrams accompanying lessons 5, 8, 10 and 12 are
taken from Athole Still's 'Flicker-Stop Books', Wolfe Publica-
tions, and those accompanying lessons 1, 2, 3 and 4 were drawn
by Donald Wilson.

Diagrams

9

Part 1

Prologue

One man knelt in prayer. Another vomited silently into a towel.
The strain showed less dramatically but just as clearly on the
faces of the other five young men who were sitting or lying on
the steel beds in the brightly-lit, bare-walled room. I remember
asking myself whether my own appearance was as calm and
confident as I wanted it to be, or whether I too was visibly a
victim of the tension, in spite of being older and more experienced than any of my seven companions.

Almost before the thought had registered, however, I realized
that the time for gamesmanship, with its confident façades, had
long since gone. This was it. The chips were down and in a few
minutes someone would pick them up in the form of an Olympic gold medal.

For me the forthcoming final of the 100 metres freestyle at
the Mexico Olympics would be the end of the road. I knew
that, win or lose, I would never again experience the atmosphere of stress which precedes such events, a thought which
surprisingly filled me with a kind of comforting nostalgia that
seemed to make me a little more composed than I had any right
to be in such company. I felt rather pleased also, as I looked
round the room, that alone of the eight finalists I had already
achieved something special in being there. None of my rivals
had previously competed in an Olympic final, whereas four years
earlier in Tokyo I had won a silver medal in this same event.
Few sprinters had ever managed to maintain form from one
Olympic Games to the next, especially in the harsh climate

of modern competitive swimming. Would any of my companions emulate this achievement at Munich in 1972?

The brightly-coloured track-suits, incongruous in the distinctly un-festive atmosphere of the room, helped me pick out the three Americans, two Russians, one Australian and one Argentinian, who with myself – Robert Bilsland McGregor, twenty-four years old, from Falkirk – would soon be challenging for one of the world's greatest sporting prizes. Normally at this stage of a major competition I avoided thinking about the race itself and my rivals, for that part of my mental preparation, together with my race planning, was usually completed well before I arrived at the pool. But on this occasion, in the shadow of many training difficulties in the immediate past, I drew considerable confidence from making a futuristic assessment of the other finalists.

The three Americans were the first to be excluded from my Munich 1972 final. It wasn't that Mark Spitz, Zac Zorn or Ken Walsh lacked class, but the past had shown it was almost impossible for an American sprinter to survive four years at the top in the United States. Zorn and Walsh would have finished their college studies before 1972, and without the advantages of the university training and competition system they would have even less chance.

Spitz presented a slightly more difficult case. Still only eighteen and not yet at college, although several of the top schools were clamouring to sign him on an athletics scholarship, he could still be near the top in 1972. However, he was not basically a sprinter, and although at that moment he was undoubtedly the world's leading swimmer, I saw his development coming in the longer freestyle distances and on the butterfly. Nor could I avoid thinking that if Don Schollander, my conqueror in Tokyo, could not hold his American Olympic sprint position from one Games to the next, then neither could Mark Spitz.

Although neither Leonid Ilichev nor Georgi Kulikov were as gifted as any of the Americans, I nevertheless found it less easy to reject them. This was a matter of politics rather than sporting ability. Being only twenty and twenty-one years old respectively, they had no major drawback in terms of age, but their greatest advantage lay in the system which they enjoyed in their homeland. Unlike most Western sportsmen, including the Americans, the Russians would not be beset by career problems during the most crucial years of their professional development. The State would take good care of them however much time they devoted to sport to the neglect of their studies. In spite of this, however, they would almost certainly succumb to the natural desire to free themselves from the constant discipline of hard training, which both had already endured for several years, and which I myself had found a major problem.

Luis Nicolao, the Argentinian, failed my 'qualifying test' simply because I thought he had already surpassed himself in reaching the present final. I had the greatest respect for him as a swimmer, however, for he had held the world's sprint butterfly record four years before and had nearly reached the butterfly final in Tokyo.

It was significant that I was considering last the tough and immensely fit Australian, Mike Wenden. Try as I could, I found it impossible to examine him as objectively as the others. He was the only man in the line-up whom I had never beaten – indeed he had beaten me two years earlier for the Commonwealth title in Jamaica. With him my thoughts rebounded sharply from Munich to Mexico City. For the first time in my life before an important race I was looking at one of my rivals with a feeling that I was looking at the winner.

This did not alarm me nearly as much as I might have expected. In fact, I felt quite relieved. Wenden had to be the strong favourite for the gold medal, and nobody wanted to be favourite here. His 51·7-second split in the team race showed him to be apparently beyond anyone else at these Games, and yet the pressures of this particular Olympic final could upset even the strongest favourite. He ought to be capable of 52·4 seconds from a dead start, a fifth of a second inside the world record held jointly by Zorn and Walsh. But only once in the history of the Olympics had a world record been set in this final – though it was an Australian, Jon Henricks, who did it then in 1956.

Thought and counter-thought filled my mind, till I pulled myself together and concentrated hard on a scene I knew well – the living-room of my home in Falkirk. It would be the middle of the night in Britain, but I knew that my parents would still be awake, listening to the radio, waiting for news from Mexico. I relaxed completely as my mind mused happily and thankfully over the good fortune which had given me, in my parents, roots as solid and fruitful as anyone could ever wish for.

I. The Beginning

For me the beginning could be said to have taken place some eight years before I was born, and more than a thousand miles from my birthplace. Berlin in 1936 may have been for many the beginning of the end in political terms, but to one tough, proud young Scot, it brought an experience so exhilarating that much . of the next thirty years of his life was to be spent in trying to recapture it in even fuller measure. The Olympic Games were being held in that city, and Davie McGregor was in the British water-polo team, which performed well in the tournament. Sporting achievements figured prominently in the McGregor family tree, and although my father was in a way at the top of the tree the other branches were also well adorned. My paternal grandfather, Robert McGregor, had also been a first-class swimmer and water-polo player and had founded the Fairfield Swimming Club in Govan, Glasgow, before the turn of the century. All his seven sons excelled in sport. The youngest, my uncle Grant McGregor, played first-class junior football, and the eldest, Robert McGregor, captained the Greenock Morton team which beat Glasgow Rangers in the 1922 Scottish Cup Final. Jimmy McGregor also reached the Cup Final, playing for St. Mirren, also against Rangers, and another brother, Alex, is generally agreed to have been the best footballer in the family, although he never played beyond the junior grade. On my mother's side there is less evidence of sporting ability, although she herself was a competitive runner in her younger days. In the face of the McGregors' formidable physical talents, however, she mustered her forces on another front, and family legend has it that soon after my parents were married, my mother was resolutely asserting that the McGregors needed Stirling blood to introduce some brains and artistic talent into the strain!

With such athletic antecedents, therefore, it was fairly predictable that one or two sporting genes would find their way into the new arrival in the McGregor household in April 1944. Displaying even in embryo the pride in performance which later became one of my basic characteristics, I refused to arrive on April Fool's Day, as expected, but kept everyone waiting not one day, but two – just to be safe! My six-year-old sister, Betty, was later to be very grateful for the arrival of a son in the family, as she had little interest in playing football and water-polo!

But my father was not hell-bent on making his son a sports champion, whether his unsuspecting offspring wanted to be one or not. Certainly, with his great love of sport and of swimming in particular, he was keen that I should excel at games, but never did he impose his will upon me to tackle something for his own gratification. I can state this quite categorically with regard to my adolescent and adult life which I can clearly remember, but obviously it is much more difficult or indeed impossible for me to speak for the earlier formative years. It must be significant, however, that although I was the son of a pool superintendent I was not taught to swim until I was nine years old. This hardly seems the behaviour of an over-ambitious father, and but for this forbearance, I doubt if my life would so happily have taken the direction it did. The freedom of will which he allowed me was a major factor in my lasting seven years at the top of international competitive swimming.

In fact it was only as a result of two unrelated adolescent passions that I began to swim at all and that, once swimming, I was given the necessary impetus to train hard. My first love, angling, remains as dear to me now as it was then, but the second did not survive my fickle adolescence.

When I was four the family moved from Helensburgh to Falkirk, where my father took over the local swimming-pool.

There were many good fishing stretches in the vicinity and when at the age of nine I showed a real keenness for this activity my parents insisted, for my own safety, that I learn to swim. My father was obviously pleased to have this excuse to make me swim and he was delighted when I picked it up very quickly. He immediately recognized my natural ability for the sport, but still he did not force me to join the training squad, which he had always formed at each of the pools where he had been employed.

Between the ages of nine and fourteen my enthusiasm found its happiest outlet in football, and if the fortune-teller at a visiting carnival had forecast an international sports career for me, we would have expected it to be on the soccer pitch and nowhere else. I loved the game, and captained my primary school team. My memories of those years are dominated by visits to many professional league games and by long happy hours playing with my school mates or practising the finer arts of the game with my father, who gave me tremendous encouragement, in one of the local parks.

Swimming was not completely neglected, however, and being the son of the local bathmaster it was expected that I should be better than most boys of my age. I 'trained' only once a week at the pool, but this was enough to put me comfortably into the school team, and before leaving primary school I did manage to win my first title of any importance, when I became champion of the Falkirk schools over 50 yards freestyle. But even this was not enough to divert my attentions from Saturday mornings with the school football team, Saturday afternoons at one of the league grounds, and Saturday nights dreaming of heading in the last-minute winner for Scotland at Wembley.

At about this time the second passion of my early life set in motion the chain of events which was to change the pattern of my existence so completely. My father had long been aware of my outstanding natural ability in the water, and also that my physique was tailor-made for high-speed swimming. He was, therefore, delighted when I asked him to enter me for my first-ever championship event, the Western District 50 yards free-style for boys under fifteen years of age. I had slightly increased my weekly swimming training, not because of any great love of hard work, but because I was extremely keen on a very attractive twelve-year-old girl, who was a good swimmer and a regular member of my father's training squad. She was also entered for her section of the Western District Championship and I knew she would be competing on the same day.

My father was well aware of my fancy and he rightly assumed that I would like to shine in her eyes. He thought this was unlikely, however, for he had agreed to my entry only because he expected me to be well beaten, due to my lack of training. The inevitable defeat, he reasoned, might make me turn to swimming with real diligence, for he felt certain, even then, that with proper application I could make the highest grade. My football talents did not strike him as having nearly the same potential. (I like to think, however, that I was something more than a 'big, daft, centre-half', as he often described me!)

When the championship eventually came along, I nearly ruined his calculations, for I was third in the final, but only 0·2 seconds behind the winner.

The shame of this defeat, the first I had ever suffered in public, was vastly increased by the presence of my girl-friend, who aggravated my frustration by becoming champion of her age group for girls. My pride was wounded, and especially at the thought of being, in my mind anyway, the inferior partner in our relationship.

Soon after the race my father was by my side with some well-chosen words of consolation. 'Dinna worry, Bobby. You swam well. It's just that these other two laddies are a bit better than you.' Only my father could have known the effect these words would have on me. He knew me as well as he knew himself, for I really was my father's son in respect of competitiveness and refusal to accept defeat. 'Better than me,' I thought. 'I'll damned well show them!' From that moment on, I was a daily attender at my father's training class.

That was the first great turning-point in my life. I have often asked myself what would have happened if I had won my race on that occasion. It is likely that I would have accepted victory as a matter of course, as I had done at primary school, and gone back to my beloved football. I was at an age when I was about to begin playing junior football, and, bearing in mind my family background and connections, I might well have been noticed by some professional club. Had that happened there would certainly have been no question of my training for swimming, or indeed of returning to swimming, if I had not made the grade on the football pitch. When I do day-dream about what might have been, however, it still ends up with my heading the winning goal for Scotland in the dying seconds at Wembley!

II. The Competitive Urge

There are more than two thousand active swimming clubs in Great Britain and they are without question the power-house of British swimming. The leading officials are in the first instance club officials, and our leading swimmers have always been produced by individual clubs, a state of affairs very different from the state sponsorship of many countries and the college system of the United States. And so it was at club level that my first regular races within the British competitive organization took place.

I was now training regularly but doing less work than many other swimmers at my own level, a situation which persisted throughout my career. There were several reasons for this. I was not lazy but I found that my personality was not of the type which could accept hour after hour of drudgery which swimming training, even in the late 1950s, was beginning to demand. In addition to this my father had decided that my build and natural technique lent themselves to sprinting, which required less sheer mileage in training. And, finally, we were agreed that, come what may, my academic studies should never suffer for a sport which, unlike football, had no professional or career possibilities.

I was good at art and mathematics, almost alone amongst my school subjects, and I had decided to try to become an architect, which I knew would mean hard studying for six years after leaving school. My father allowed these factors to dominate our preparations for competition and he therefore gave a great deal of attention to my stroke technique, so that whatever training we did would be put to the most efficient use.

The fact that I was not the most prolific swimmer in terms of training loads was initially a two-edged blessing. By working less than others I was obliged to swim technically very well in order to maintain a good level of performance. This was a great advantage. But on the few occasions when I was defeated early in my career, almost invariably by older and more experienced opponents, I had a built-in excuse – 'After all, I'm not training as hard as they are'. I detested defeat, but I was nevertheless more of a 'wishbone' swimmer than a 'backbone' one. I remember saying to my father one day that I wished I could swim as fast as the club champion. 'Son, this swimmer looks good to you, but in Glasgow he's a second-rater and in London he's a non-starter. If you want to do anything at all with your life, aim for the top. Be positive. Work harder.'

His words struck home and I put more effort into my training, although the greatest change came in my attitude to competition. There was no longer a 'wish' complex. Even in defeat I would consciously say to myself, 'He's beaten me this time, but I'm aiming for the top'.

Success at club level was soon followed by victories in the Western District championship, which I had narrowly missed the previous year, and in the Scottish Schools' 100 yards freestyle championship. I was beginning to have my first publicity in the local paper and how I enjoyed it! At barely fifteen years of age I was considered important enough to be mentioned in the press, and, indeed, for my photograph to be published. Looking back, I realize that this was important to me, and I have come to believe that most successful *amateur* sportsmen, and many professionals also, are impelled by a basic inferiority complex. They *must* do well – and be seen to do well in order to compensate for other deficiencies. This was the case with me, and although it may seem improbable in someone who was naturally gifted, I was also shy and rather introspective. It is difficult to

be objective and accurate about one's own character, but my
sense of inadequacy probably had its origins in my only
average performance at school work, where I would dearly have
liked to excel.

As I grew older, so I trained harder and success followed
success, although still at a regional level. For the first time I
began to experience real pain in my training exertions, and this
helped to expose even further the highly competitive streak
which I had inherited from my father and the McGregor
family. Games of table-tennis or water-polo took on a new
meaning for me. I still enjoyed playing them, but now I tried
hard to win even in fun games, and I felt I was letting myself
down when I didn't.

By 1960, when I was sixteen, I was the fastest swimmer in the
West of Scotland, and our club, Falkirk Otters, was setting the
pace for clubs all over Scotland. My father had done a fine job.
The whole squad thought the world of him and the happy
atmosphere of training sessions did a great deal to bring the very
best out of us. The fact that I was a member of a fairly large
group helped also to eliminate many of the difficulties which
occur when a parent is also the coach. One learnt to accept
without question what 'the boss' put forward as the best group
policy, and fortunately this attitude remained with me long
after I had outstripped my training companions. The respect for
one another which my father and I built up at this time never
showed any signs of cracking in later years, even when we were
under severe physical and psychological stress.

As we moved into the 1960s, my outlook underwent another
significant change. My intention of 'aiming for the top' was still
in the forefront of my mind, but partly because of my increasing
success and partly because of my growing maturity, I began to
realize that 'the top' was a relative term. Until then my goal,
although I had never specified it to myself, would almost certainly have been achieved when I had satisfied the emotional
and traditionally Scottish desire to annihilate the English! But
why stop there, I began to ask? The world was large, with many

fields to conquer, notably the Olympic ones. For the first time my ambitions became formalized, I wanted the ultimate sporting accolade of an Olympic gold medal.

I can remember exactly the circumstances of my 'conversion'. It was the spring of 1960 and the sports pages were already beginning to feature previews and assessments of the forth-coming Olympic Games in Rome. As usual the name of Ian Black figured prominently. No other single sportsman had a greater effect on me during my early competitive years than this superbly fit and talented Scottish schoolboy. For two years he had epitomized all that was good in the British way of sport, and was deservedly the nation's outstanding athlete between 1958 and 1960. It was Black who made me realize that there was no limit to what could be achieved, and as I read of his exploits in the national dailies I began to feel that, if he could do it, so could I.

Up to this point the Olympics had been mentioned in con-versations between my father and myself only when we were discussing other sportsmen, or my father's own participation in Berlin in 1936. But one evening in May 1960, I threw out the first feeler: 'Dad, do you think I could ever swim in the Olympics?' Before he could utter a word in reply my mother had countered with, 'Now don't be silly, Bobby. You know you'll have your architectural studies. Won't he, Davie?' My father gave his well-known, non-committal, 'Mm,' which meant, according to its pitch, that he either agreed with my mother, but didn't feel like continuing the conversation, or that he disagreed with her, but was reluctant to become involved in an argument. My well-trained ear told me that it was the latter case, so I pressed on. 'If Black can do it, why can't I?' There was silence, my mother looked anxiously at my father and I knew from her expression that they at least were not coming fresh to the subject. 'Of course, son, I've always thought you could. And you could win the sprint too,' exploded my father defiantly, as my mother nervously and needlessly busied herself with the crockery as the best mothers and wives do when they know that their token resistance has failed and that the decision must be left to the men.

The absence of doubt in my father's last words filled me with a real excitement, as he had always been the 'typical' Scot in not saying too much, and he had certainly never before been so specific in what he thought of my ability. I had always received plenty of encouragement from him, but as often as he had urged me on, he had also warned me, unnecessarily I hope, of the dangers of becoming 'big-headed', and his compliments were therefore usually couched in generalizations. Now his cards were well and truly on the table, but the significant feature of this unique episode in our relationship was the fact that he had waited until I called his hand.

My mother had played her usual protective role. Her initial opposition was motivated, not by lack of confidence in my ability, but a typically maternal desire to shelter her son from several years of extreme discipline. She herself is the most un-competitive of individuals, and the thought of my being exposed to the stresses and strains of constant training and competition, with their inevitable disappointments, was more than she could accept without comment.

There was also, however, the more practical and obvious cause of her reluctance. Both she and my father wanted me to be well qualified professionally. They were well aware that many young men fail to prepare themselves adequately for a good career by over-indulgence in sport and they did not want this to happen with me. We all agreed that concessions to my studies would have to be made in the following years, and this was the overriding principle which neither my father nor I ever forgot.

III. The Ladder to the Top

Without question the happiest and most enjoyable years of my swimming career were those from 1960 to 1964. They were the years which saw my rise from local to international competitions, and throughout that period I was driven by an insatiable desire to reach the top – to prove I was the best. They were the most interesting and exciting years also because everything was new for me. In 1960 I was a very naïve sixteen-year-old, who had never ventured far from the west of Scotland; in 1964 I returned from Tokyo as a mature young man, widely travelled, fairly sophisticated and with an awareness of what life demands of those who seek success. But more of that later.

My father and I both realized that if we were to have any international success, as a first step, I would have to take my chances against the best in Scotland and then in England. I use the 'we' intentionally because our relationship achieved the ultimate in understanding between the coach and athlete. We knew each other to an almost telepathic degree and I have always found it impossible to think of my assault on the swimming world as being anything but a joint effort.

A few months after our decision, I successfully negotiated the first national hurdle, when I won the Scottish junior 100 yards freestyle championship. It was a moment of real celebration for the family, and we were particularly pleased because I won easily and my time of 55·5 seconds was faster than all but the first three in the senior race. Unofficially, therefore, I could consider myself one of the fastest sprinters in Scotland, although my father did not allow me to make too much of this, quickly pointing out that I still had a long way to go.

Nevertheless, the knowledge that I was the fastest swimmer of my age in Scotland gave me a marvellous fillip, and for some time afterwards my training became sheer joy, no matter how hard it was. This raises an interesting point.

The question most asked of any successful swimmer is – 'Why do you have to be young to shine at swimming?' The truth of the matter is that you don't have to be young at all. In fact, if certain other factors could be duplicated much later in life, then most of our outstanding swimmers would be in their late twenties or even early thirties, when a man is probably at his physical peak; but it is because these 'other factors' are seldom found later in life that the balance is tipped heavily in favour of the young. For swimming differs from most other sports in three distinct ways: (1) it can (and should, for safety's sake) be practised when very young and because there is no contact with physical objects there is no danger whatever of damage being done to a young, growing body; (2) technique is enormously important, for the obvious reason that we are dealing with a much denser medium than in any other sport, and a lack of technical efficiency in terms of streamlining can impose intolerable disadvantages on the performer; (3) fitness is much more important than sheer strength.

It is clear that a child can fulfil these prerequisites just as easily as an adult – but certainly no more easily. Why, then, do so many of the world's leading swimmers come from the teenage age group? The answer lies in the social and psychological 'other factors' which I mentioned earlier.

The first is the question of time available for training. It is generally agreed that more time is required to prepare for top-class swimming performance than any other sport. I do not say that swimmers train *harder* than other sportsmen, but international swimming standards are set by the Americans and Australians, who regularly train in excess of five hours daily. No one, however naturally gifted he may be, can hope to achieve a significant international ranking on less than three hours' work daily, and only a technically outstanding sprinter could get by on that little. How many young men could possibly spare that amount of time in their mid-twenties? These are the years when the foundations of a successful business or professional career are being laid, and only a very small percentage of young men would want to prejudice the rest of their lives for the sake of an amateur sport.

At about the same age, of course, young women are preparing for marriage and children and these basic natural desires supersede all others. School-children, and students, therefore, with their comparatively short and not physically strenuous working day, form perhaps the only group which can consider undertaking the training necessary for international competition.

The final factor which gives the young a great advantage in most areas of human endeavour lies in the great natural enthusiasm which we all experience at adolescence. We become so involved and single-minded in the things we enjoy that little else seems to matter and even the hardest work seems to pass unnoticed. Of course there are many sports where this factor would not be enough – tennis, golf, soccer, rugby, and so on – because in those sports strength and, indeed, size are important, but this is not the case with swimming.

To sum up, if swimmers in their twenties could spend enough time training and if they could maintain a real enthusiasm for their sport, then they and not the teenagers would be the world's outstanding swimmers. But modern society being what it is, I doubt whether this will ever be proved.

These are some of the reasons why I found my increased training loads really enjoyable in the summer of 1960. Everything was going with a swing. Life was good, as I prepared for my next big challenge, the 100 yards freestyle for juniors at the Amateur Swimming Association championships in Blackpool. There were, of course, the English Championships, but being open to all British swimmers, and, indeed to the whole world, they are usually described as the 'British Championships'.

And so, in August 1960, I left Scotland for the first time in my life to tackle the 'auld enemy' on his home ground. Although I was already quite well known within the sport in Scotland, I was a novice in English eyes, which was an advantage to me as an up-and-coming young sportsman. The first time that one competes at a slightly higher level than before little is expected, and therefore a reputation can only be made, never lost. This goes a long way towards relieving the pressures which can adversely affect one's performance in an important event.

Blackpool and the Derby baths during 'Nationals Week' provide a fascinating and unique experience. Upwards of 1,500 competitors with a similar number of supporters so monopolize the boarding-houses on the front that a half-mile stretch, from the Imperial Hotel in the South to the Cliffs Hotel in the North, with its immediate hinterland, becomes a swimming utopia. The only qualifications for admission are a suitably emblazoned track-suit and a boundless desire to eat, drink and sleep swimming.

The A.S.A. championships are a swimmer's baptism and only when one has made the pilgrimage and undergone complete immersion in this swimming community does one become a fully-fledged member. I presented myself with trepidation. I expected to find the English as fragrantly anti-Scottish as I was anti-them, and although this did not worry me with regard to the competitions, I was not looking forward to the social antagonism which I felt would be inevitable. To my surprise I was made to feel completely at home, and I soon discovered that, perhaps due to the inborn sense of superiority which allegedly pervades all Englishmen, they were much more worried about each other than about any foreigners, be they from just north of the border or from much further afield. The greatest rivalry was between the factions from the north of England and from the south. Both derived great satisfaction from any defeat of the other, which they vociferously spelled out in their respective battle-chants after each event. Generally speaking the Scots came out best of all as far as applause was concerned, for they were always well supported by the north of England contingent, which considers that all the decent Britons are born north of Potters Bar! Southern supporters would also applaud the Scots, but with the condescending sense of superiority which seems to be characteristic of them.

Blackpool also brought my introduction to the gamesmanship which is only a short head behind swimming as the most popular pastime of the week. Some of it was amusing, such as the laboured nonchalance of one young swimmer who was seldom seen without an empty beer can in his hand and a cigarette behind his ear, although he neither smoked nor drank. Some was more sinister, like the sprinter who took off his track-suit alongside his most dangerous opponent and 'accidentally' dropped a hypodermic syringe. And some quite hilarious, such as the two fourteen-year-old girl rivals, of impeccable upbringing, perpetrating impossible lies about their best performances with a glib, barefacedness that would have made a politician blush!

I kept pretty much to myself throughout the week and tried not to be involved in these 'war games'. Luckily my father had put me wise to them in advance, and any comments or behaviour aimed at unsettling me certainly had no effect. I qualified for the final of my only event, the boys 110 yards freestyle, and finished third in 60·8 seconds, the same time as Ken Brown (York) in second place, but well beaten by the young English sprinter Peter Hammond, of Sheffield, with a winning time of 59 seconds dead.

My own performance indicated an improvement of about one second on my Scottish championship swim, and from that point of view I was well pleased with it. I happened to mention to my father that it would have been nice to finish second, particularly as I had the same time as my immediate victor. He looked at me with the inscrutable expression of which he has always been a master. 'Perhaps. But don't forget, first is first and second's nowhere.'

A couple of years before, after my defeat in my first West of

Scotland championship, he had cast his lure with magnificent accuracy. Now, knowing I was well and truly hooked, he was playing me beautifully.

My defeat and my father's words had exactly the right affect on me at exactly the right time. My reaction might well have been to crawl back to Falkirk with thoughts of curtailing my giant-killing to Scotland. Nothing was further from my mind. I could hardly wait to get home to start my winter training, and many, many times, as I ploughed a lonely furrow up and down the pool at seven o'clock on a cold winter's morning, did my mind drift back to that race at the Derby baths. I would play a game with myself, imagining that the last ten yards of a particularly tiring training repetition was the last few yards of my next race against Peter Hammond, and, needless to say, I invariably managed to pull out just enough to touch home first!

For the first time my father included weight-training in my winter schedules and the beneficial results were immediately apparent when I began to do some fairly high-quality time trials at the beginning of 1961. I had gained a great deal of shoulder strength, which is particularly important to a sprinter, and by the spring I was already swimming faster than ever before, although the season had barely started. All the signs pointed to some fine swimming throughout the year and I was spurred on by the knowledge that Ian Black had apparently retired, or at least was showing no signs of competing, which made my chances of international selection for Scotland a distinct possibility.

My performances in 1960 had not escaped the notice of the British selectors and in April 1961 I was invited to take part in the international trials which open each season.

They were to be held in Walsall and I set off with the happy knowledge that on last year's form none of the other competitors would expect me to finish much higher than eighth. My father and I knew, however, that I was swimming more than a second faster than my A.S.A. performance, and although neither of us expected me to finish in the first three, nevertheless, a personal best time seemed likely.

1. A mixture of shock and delight as I am told my time for a 50-yard record attempt at our club gala in 1962. It was my first Scottish record and my first genuinely international-class performance (22·2 seconds)

2a. The man behind it all –
my father, David McGregor

2b. The happy training squad at Falkirk's Otter Swimming Club.
This must have been taken *before* a training session!

As usual I was swimming in only one event, the 100 yards freestyle, and for the first time in my life I lined up with the 'big boys' of England, Stan Clark (Plaistow), Peter Kendrew (York), and Bill O'Donnell (Eccles), all full Great Britain internationals, and the last-named the only Briton to break the magic 50-seconds barrier over 100 yards. In addition both my Blackpool conquerors, Hammond and Brown, had qualified, along with two other well-known seniors.

The race went much as expected, with the big three finishing in the above order, but in fourth place, one-tenth of a second ahead of Peter Hammond, came R. B. McGregor! I was delighted with my best-ever time of 59·5 seconds, and even more with my defeat of Hammond, for the closing stages of the race had gone exactly as I had imagined in my many make-believe duels with the British junior champion during my winter training.

I was unworried by the fact that Clarke's winning time seemed a distant 57·6 seconds, because my father had conditioned me to realize that the jump from junior to senior was a critical one, and although we always aimed to win, we had to be realistic in relation to my first senior swim against three experienced men, when I was only a few weeks past my seventeenth birthday.

Being a sprinter, with no aspirations to go over the distance, I did not compete in the 220 yards freestyle, which always formed the basis for selection of the 4 × 220 yards freestyle team which in those days was the only freestyle team event. But I was considerably encouraged by the knowledge that if there had been a 4 × 110 yards relay, which almost everyone was then advocating, I would have had my first British 'cap'.

Yet I still had not swum for Scotland! I did not, however, have long to wait. Within a few days of returning from Walsall I had been invited to represent a Scotland/Wales v. England v. France at Coatbridge in August. The whole family was jubilant, for selection for Scotland really did come before everything else. My father and I set about trying to make my début a successful one.

C

The whole of the 1961 season went marvellously for me from then on. In the absence of Ian Black I romped home an easy winner in the senior Scottish championship in July, and in August I won the 100 yards in the triangular international match, defeating the French champion Gropaiz and England's Jeff Allan. This victory did not register with me as much as it might have, for although my time of 52·8 seconds was again an improvement on my previous best, I had already beaten Allan in the international trials and I knew there were at least three English sprinters better than he. For me the final and major test of the season would be the Bologna Trophy event between Scotland, England and Wales. I intended to miss the British championships in order to take a September holiday, a break which I found increasingly necessary and beneficial, as the years went on, and this meant I would not be able to match my improving ability against the hard-core English sprinting strength until the Bologna Contest in October. When it finally came I was well rested, fit, and delighted that Peter Kendrew, one of the established stars, was the English selection. The match at Coatbridge was as much a disaster for Scotland as it was a triumph for me, for I won the 100 yards event, the only Scottish victory, in yet another personal best time of 52 seconds dead. But more important to me than the time was the fact that Peter Kendrew, the best opponent England could muster, finished behind me.

That day stands out in my memory as the time when I clearly saw that I really could be the best in Britain – and more. Eighteen months earlier my father had stated his belief in me, and I had set about trying to live up to it. But since the task we had set ourselves was an ambitious one, there were inevitably moments of doubt even in the midst of success, and I had had my fair share of them in the previous two seasons. The Bologna result swept them out of my mind for now I *knew* there was nothing that should stop me moving on to the highest international level. I finished the season impatiently looking forward to 1962.

IV. In the Shadow of Black

My progress in 1961 had been made easier by the fact that Britain's greatest ever swimmer, Ian Black, had not been competing. Although primarily a middle-distance man and butterflier, his class and fitness were such that he was also a daunting opponent on the sprint, and he still held the Scottish 110 yards record with a long-course (i.e. 50-metre or 55-yard pool) time of 58 seconds, set in 1959 when he won the British title. Rumour now had it that he was again carrying out tremendous training loads, doing much more sprint work, and would make a powerful comeback. What I was up against was strikingly displayed in my father's own pool on 14 April, when Black was guest of honour at our annual club swimming gala. He looked superbly fit and heavily muscled as a result of a great deal of winter weight training. But the muscle was not of the disproportionate, bulky, body-builder's variety. On him it seemed to mould perfectly with the contours of his body, so that he presented the appearance of a beautifully-streamlined miniature torpedo. (Among swimmers he was well below average in height, 5 ft. 9 in.) The mere sight of him would have been enough to intimidate most opponents and it came as no surprise to me, after I had watched him speed up and down my home waters, that he had smashed all his own British and Scottish records for the 220 yard freestyle with a magnificent swim of 2 minutes 03·8 seconds, which was only 2·2 seconds outside the world record of the Australian, Jon Konrads.

Black had a deserved reputation for being brusque and unapproachable and he certainly lived up to it on this occasion. I made a hesitant and self-conscious attempt at conversation, but my words seemed barely to register.

The natives of the Northern Highlands are usually considered by other Scots to be deep, introspective and suspicious of strangers, instincts bred in the dreadful days of persecution during the Stewart uprisings and the Highland Clearances. Black was a typical 'Hielander' and, apart from his swimming, the only quality with which I sympathized at our first meeting was his well-known hatred of all things English. With his tartan bath robe, towel, slippers and trunks, and ultra-confident air, he might well have been Bonnie Prince Charlie returned to claim his rightful throne, and the crowd rose to him with wild enthusiasm. *My* crowd, in *my* pool. I felt slightly deflated by a mixture of injured pride, rage, and envy, but I soon pulled myself together for my own challenge. I was billed to attempt the Scottish 50-yard record of 23 seconds held by Jockie McDonald of Inverness. It was a really good record, reflecting a much higher standard than McDonald was capable of over the internationally-accepted 100 yards. As it turned out, however, my reaction to Black's superb performance was an excellent one from myself. I sped over the two lengths and touched home in 22·2 seconds, for the first world-class performance of my career. Even in the United States, the traditional home of top-class sprinters, where this distance is a national championship, my time would have ranked with the best.

I was elated not so much because of my performance, but more because I felt I had made an appropriate, indeed the *only* appropriate, reply to Black's apparent aloofness. Just how great an effect my swim had on Black was to be shown before long.

During the gala my father had had the opportunity of talking with Black's coach, Andy Robb, who had a formidable record for producing champions. He was similar to my father in many respects. He was also a former water-polo player turned teacher and pool superintendent, and behind the same dark weather-beaten face lurked the same clinical, reticent nature. There were many who considered the conversational confrontation between these two to be the real highlight of the gala. After the initial skirmishing, which lasted two hours and involved the exchange of about half a dozen words and an unknown number of shrugs and nods and enough 'mms', 'ahs', 'achs' and 'ayes', at differing voice pitches to write an opera, they finally got down to the in-fighting and by the end of the evening it appeared that my father had won on a split decision. He had interpreted that Black intended to make his main bid of the season in November for the Commonwealth Games in Perth, Australia, and that he was definitely going for the sprint in addition to his usual events. Robb, of course, had been at a considerable disadvantage, because there was nothing to find out about me, it being well known that I had no intention of moving up from the 110 yards, and my swimming form was clear to anyone with a stop-watch.

The thought of meeting Ian Black on level terms no longer filled me with dismay, but the task I had set myself a few months earlier was now obviously harder. I conceded him the first round of the season for the sheer impact and quality of his come-back, but I looked forward with excitement and determination to round two, which was to take place the following Saturday.

The trials to select the nucleus of the Scottish Commonwealth Games team and the qualifiers for the British Trials in May were being held in Rosyth. We knew that Black was making a 110 yards freestyle record attempt two weeks later in Inverness, and as he must have been in sprinting condition we expected him to line up for the 110 at Rosyth, but instead he elected to cruise through a leisurely 440. This made me feel quite good as I reasoned (correctly, I discovered later) that he was not keen to meet me on sprinting territory yet. I won the 110 in 57·4 seconds, clipping ·6 seconds off Black's Scottish record, and was pleased to think that once again I had improved on my previous best performance. But a nagging doubt remained in my mind about Black's real sprint form, as the second man to me in the 110 did 57·8 seconds. This was Athole Still, an experienced

Scottish and British representative and Black's training companion. He was, like myself, a 'pure' sprinter, and although never given to modesty he dismissed his performance as mediocre, saying that Black was thrashing him on sprint work in training.

I realized, of course, that this could well have been 'stable' talk, but Still's own performance was the first time he had officially beaten 58 seconds, and as he, like Black, had not been competing since 1960, it certainly indicated that something was brewing in Aberdeen.

However, having apparently frightened Black out of competing in the sprint and then having relieved him of one of his records, I felt justified in claiming the second round in our long-range psychological battle.

The following week I travelled down to Blackpool for the British International Trials. They were being held in two sessions which necessitated my swimming a 110 yards freestyle in each of them, and the team would be selected on the basis of both performances.

I was delighted when I won the first sprint in a British long-course best of 57·4 seconds and I knew my selection was therefore guaranteed unless I flopped in the second race.

As we came under starter's orders the second time, Stan Clarke walked towards me, his face wreathed in smiles and his huge, clenched fist reaching out to me, as if offering me something. I stretched out my open palm and a baby's teat dropped into it. The inference was obvious, but I was not put off. I laid the teat beside my block and took up my starting position. Fifty-seven point three seconds later, after romping home a comfortable winner, I ducked under the lane ropes and made my way towards Clarke. As usual he was grinning, even in defeat, and he offered his hand to congratulate me. My own moved forward also, but I clasped his only after I had planted the baby's teat squarely between his lips, much to the amusement of the other competitors, judges and time-keepers.

It had been a great day for me and I looked forward immensely to the opening of my international career in June, when Britain had an away match with East Germany and a home one with West Germany.

On paper it seemed as if my first major goal had been reached – I was Britain's fastest swimmer. But was I? Black had not swum in the trials at all, as he had his final university exams in June and therefore did not want to be considered for the international matches in that month. The thought that Black might be able to beat me became an obsession and I thought of him constantly as I trained, trying to will myself into a confident attitude for our inevitable encounter. In spite of some feelings of doubt, however, logic told me that Black had never officially swum as fast as I had, and on that reasoning I happily chalked up round three to myself, feeling at heart quietly confident that I was a clear leader on points.

Over the next two weeks Black delivered a wicked 'one-two' which left not only myself, but many of the world's leading swimmers, gasping on the ropes. At Inverness, his birthplace, he smashed the British 110-yard record with a startling 55·5 seconds swim, which was only 0·9 seconds off the world record of the 1960 Olympic Gold medallist, Australian John Devitt. Although Black's swim had the advantage of two extra turns, as he was an experienced long-course swimmer and not a particularly good turner it seemed likely that he would reproduce this form in an internationally acceptable pool. His performance seemed all the more frightening too, since he had achieved it in a solo time trial, without the competitive incentive on which he thrived.

The following week he surpassed even this performance with new British and European records over 220 yards in the Cardiff long-course pool. His time of 2 minutes 2·5 seconds was only one second outside Jon Konrad's world record, and at half-way he had been clocked at 58·5 seconds, which only myself and Stan Clarke had beaten in the British trials in the individual 110 yards event!

My father sensed how I was feeling as a result of these swims and he took a firm hold of the situation. 'Black's been five years at the top of international competition. He finds it more difficult to improve all the time, while you improve constantly as a matter of course. Forget him, and let's get on with our own work.'

My father was right, of course, I was improving all the time and a great deal could happen between now and the first time Black and I stood on the blocks together. At that time a confrontation did not seem likely before the European Games in August or possibly even the Commonwealth Games in November, for although we had both been selected for the West German match, it was considered unlikely that Black would compete, because he would be heavily involved with university examinations.

On my father's advice I centred my thoughts exclusively on doing well in my international début against East Germany in Magdeburg in the middle of June.

V. An Innocent Abroad

I looked forward to my baptism for Great Britain with a
pleasure which was heightened by the anticipation of my first
trip abroad and my first flight in an aeroplane, both exciting
prospects for a schoolboy who was not yet eighteen.

Immediately after my selection we encountered a difficulty
which was to recur at regular intervals over the next six years.
My final school exams were at the beginning of June, just before
the match with East Germany. My own reaction was the
typically adolescent one of not wanting anything to interfere
with my training for the match, but my father was much less
easily diverted from the proper priorities, and it was to my
studies and not to training that concessions were made. Much
though I realized deep down that the decision was the right one,
it was with certain misgivings that I approached the task of up-
holding Britain's honour on the Continent.

As it turned out my doubts were completely unfounded, and
indeed the episode of the exams was a twofold blessing in dis-
guise. In the first place I set off for Germany knowing that I had
done well enough academically to be sure of acceptance for an
Architectural course at the Glasgow Technical College, and
secondly the slight slackening-off in training had had the effect
of sharpening me up.

My timetable from the moment I left Falkirk before the
match until my return followed a pattern to which I became
very much accustomed over the next few years, but the impact
of this, my first international trip, was so great that a clear,

minutely-detailed picture remains with me even now, long after the memories of more recent and more glamorous experiences have vanished.

My father and I set out for Glasgow Airport at midday on the Thursday, just after I had finished the kind of meal that mothers reserve for departing only sons as a substitute for the words they seem unable to find. The atmosphere in the house was one of measured solemnity, with little talking being done by anybody, not even my usually effervescent sister, Betty. There were many occasions similar to this in later years, but nothing quite so stark. My mother could easily have accompanied us to the air-field, but it was clear that the sight of me flying off in an aero-plane would be too much for her, so a stiff-upper-lip farewell was taken on the doorstep.

There are times when living on a council estate can be irk-some, but this certainly wasn't one of them. Everybody in the street seemed to know the exact time of my departure for Glas-gow, and the ten-yard walk from the front door to the car was witnessed by smiling faces from the windows of the immediately neighbouring houses and by little groups of housewives who had moved closer from their homes further along the street. I blushed furiously and hung my head in genuine embarrassment. That these neighbours really cared and wanted to wish me well filled me with a warm feeling which brought me near to tears. It was a feeling which I came to know well, as the wonderful people of Falkirk continued to give me great support through-out the years: a support which never varied whether I was winner or loser but which apparently drew sufficient satisfac-tion from the simple knowledge that I had done my best.

As there were no other Scots in the team, I travelled alone on the hour-long flight to London, during which I had my first taste of the V.I.P. treatment which the international sportsman constantly receives. The senior steward was obviously a keen reader of the back pages of the newspapers, for he recognized me from a photograph which had appeared that day. A few minutes after take-off a delightful stewardess politely asked,

'Would you please come with me, sir?' I followed her with the ill-disguised enthusiasm which one would expect of any seventeen-year-old who had just put down a Len Deighton novel and although my wildest fantasies were not realized, I was ushered into what I later discovered was the first-class cabin, which was almost empty. The ensuing hour passed in a euphoria of soft drinks, excellent food, and ego-boosting conversations with the rest of the cabin staff, who all seemed to have been selected from the Miss World competition! I stepped off that plane at Heathrow flushed and buoyant, firmly convinced that this was the life I was meant to live, and grateful for the cabin staff's swift realization of the same fact!

The luxurious hospitality of BEA was soon followed by the equally pampering comforts of a first-class hotel in the Bayswater Road. Most of the team on that occasion came from the south of England, and would not be assembling till early the following morning, so I found myself quite alone in the hotel and sorely in need of the kind of support and advice which one of the more experienced team members could have given me. The ritual of having my bag taken to my room would have done justice to a Jerry Lewis movie. In an attempt not to appear *gauche* I had carefully thought out much of my behaviour in advance, but my preconceived notions collapsed into uncomfortable embarrassment, as an elderly, dwarf-like porter proceeded to carry my bag to the lift. I showed him in, and listened with compassion as he explained that he had a heart condition and was only taking my bag as the other porter was placing a five-shilling double across the road. I carried my own bag to the room and tipped him half-a-crown with a matter-of-fact 'Thank you' followed by my inevitable 'sir', which I just failed to smother. Such was my entry into the sweet life of the traveller.

After a few chapters of my novel I once again felt ready to face the hotel staff. I walked to the lift and was awaiting its arrival when I was joined by Anita Lonsborough. 'Hello, Bobby. You on this floor too?' 'Yes,' I replied, just managing to avoid adding the 'ma'am', which the queenly bearing of the Olympic gold medallist always seemed to command. But her first-name greeting had given me a marvellous boost and I really felt as if I 'belonged'. That may seem strange, but we had never spoken to each other before, and although I had been in her company several times, I had never felt important enough to engage her in conversation. And in case that also seems strange, let me explain that a class distinction exists in the world of sport, not based in any way on social criteria, but entirely on athletic achievement. In most cases, the distinctions are actually originated by the less successful or up-and-coming performers, who do not wish to appear 'pushy', which I suppose bears out the old adage that as often as not success changes those in contact with a successful person more than it changes that person himself.

And so with new-found confidence the young McGregor strode confidently from the lift and escorted the queen of British sport to the hotel dining-room. I felt I negotiated the always hazardous entry into a crowded room with suitable panache and the meal passed pleasantly, apart from the fact that we were the object of the smiling attentions of many of the other diners, and although I realized that this was probably because my team mate had been recognized, I nevertheless harboured a suspicion that some of the other guests might think we were a honeymoon couple!

After dinner we both watched television until Anita decided to retire at about 9.30 p.m. For me, however, the bright lights of London's West End beckoning gaudily in the distance proved a much stronger attraction than the empty whiteness of my bed-sheets, and I was soon walking briskly to the nearby tube station with the jovial words (his double must have come up) of the other porter ringing in my ears, 'Central Line, change at Oxford Circus to the Bakerloo line, southbound. One stop to Piccadilly Circus.'

I did experience some twinge of conscience, as I rattled and swung my way under London's streets instead of enjoying the sleep of the innocent in my hotel room; but this was the first time I was visiting London.

I arrived without mishap at the 'centre of the Empire' under the wings of Eros and was involuntarily caught up in the heavy phalanx of fellow sightseers, which moved slowly eastwards down Coventry Street, with the kind of haphazard regimentation, which one associates with a Latin American army column on the march. Perhaps a Foreign Legion column might be a better description, because I was immediately struck by the almost total absence of English in the snatches of multi-lingual conversation which I managed to hear.

At Leicester Square I decided to desert the column, which I did in much the same way as I left the moving staircase in the underground, slithering to a halt in a less busy side street. The little map which I had picked up in the hotel indicated that I could cut through some back streets on to Shaftesbury Avenue, and complete the triangle back to Piccadilly Circus, for my homeward journey, so on I pressed.

My thirty minutes' sojourn in Soho was the most enlightening, amusing, shocking, frightening and saddening half-hour in my young life. The luridly advertised strip-tease shows, the dingy, pimp-fronted clip joints, the painted ladies full of persistent invitation, and the countless sad-faced souls, whose wanderings there were anything but aimless, all helped to bring home to me the good fortune of my own existence. I extricated myself as quickly as my inexpert map-reading would allow, and hurried back to Piccadilly Circus.

I returned to the hotel before 11 p.m. feeling a little more adult and less innocent than I had been a short time before; and I could not resist a chuckle as I switched out the bedside light, at the effect my visit to the underworld, suitably embellished, of course, would have on the sixth form at Falkirk High School!

The rest of the team assembled next morning and we flew from London Airport to Berlin. There we transferred to a coach in which we were to complete the journey to Magdeburg by road. This meant passing through the Berlin Wall at Checkpoint Charlie, a particularly fascinating experience for someone like myself, whose favourite reading was spy stories.

There was a considerable delay at the border while passport formalities were carried out and this provided the irrepressible Stan Clarke with a golden opportunity of indulging in one of the madcap escapades which I soon realized were a feature of all the trips in which he took part. He had slipped away, and had lost no time in making his way through forbidden territory to a point in no-man's-land between the barbed wire border fences. Our attention was eventually drawn to him by the shouts of several East German guards, who at ten yards range were indicating to him with the threatening points of their rifles, that he had no right to be there. Stan's only comment was to put on a West German helmet, which he had somehow appropriated, and with a toothy grin he rejoined us beside the coach. These goings-on were unknown to the team manager, who was in the border office, but it would probably have made little difference anyway, for Stan had such an amusing personality, that his near total disregard for rules and regulations was usually pardoned. Nevertheless it is difficult to grasp that he later became a member of the Metropolitan Police!

The match opened the following day and I saw that I was due to swim in the first event against the East German champion, Frank Wiegand, who was the clear form favourite for the race. I arrived at the pool an hour before my race and spent fifteen minutes warming up. I then decided to slip into a six-by-six-foot canvas-sided plunge-bath, which stood just inside a secondary entrance to the men's changing-room. It was kept brimful by a constant flow of dark warm water from a large pipe and the surplus overflowed down the drains. I took off my trunks and jumped in, thoroughly enjoying the warm water which reached up to my neck.

I had been there only a few minutes when an East German girl diver skipped down the few steps from the poolside and rubbing her shoulders to indicate how cold she felt, smilingly jumped in beside me! I tried to hide my embarrassment, murmured a quick prayer of thanks for the dark water, and decided to beat a hasty retreat when she left.

Two minutes later, however, we were joined by another girl diver and the first one left. The change-over took place twice more and I began to think that they knew of my predicament and were enjoying themselves at my expense, but the picture suddenly became frighteningly clear. It was a rather cool, blustery day and these two were keeping warm between their practice dives by sharing my bath in rotation!

I knew no German, they had no English and I decided that sign language might land me in even worse trouble, so I resigned myself to waiting until they both left or a British swimmer came along. This never happened, however, for the main entrance to the men's changing-room was half-way down the pool, and I sat there till the divers were asked to clear the boards for the beginning of the match.

After the eventual joint departure of my two companions I had just enough time to dry myself, pull on my trunks and make my way to the start. I may have looked like a lobster, but I certainly did not swim like one, for I won the race in 56·1 seconds, which was a British best long-course performance.

VI. The King is Dead, Long Live the King

I returned from Magdeburg to find the national papers full of Britain's unexpected victory, with my own performance and photograph figuring prominently in the headlines of the Scottish editions. It seemed as if the sports writers saved their superlatives for international events, for I was variously described as a 'new swimming wonder' and the teenager who 'burst with megaton force on world swimming'! I certainly enjoyed reading these reports and the small wave of local adulation which followed, but my father made sure that my head was not even slightly turned by the exaggerations of the popular press. He threw me a copy of the previous Saturday's paper. At the bottom of one page a few lines had been circled in red. 'Ian Black, who had been expected to withdraw due to pressure of examinations, has informed the British selectors that he will swim in the match versus West Germany at Blackpool next weekend. He competes in the 110 yards and 440 yards freestyle events.' The greatest test of my swimming career was only five days away!

I wished that I had another month to prepare for the meeting with Black. I doubted that I had improved enough to beat him and I had visions of him training like a madman (as he always did), while I had eased off before going to Germany. I saw my brief reign as the king of Britain's sprinters coming to an abrupt end. But I was determined to make certain that, if my supremacy

3. But for my love of this sport, I might never have become a
champion swimmer

4a. I realize one of my early ambitions – victory in the English 110 yards freestyle championship

4b. (below) The result of the spirit at the Commonwealth Games in Perth, Australia.

Davie Dickson (Australia) the bronze medallist, grins and shows why these are called the 'happy family' Games.

Dick Pound (Canada) surveys the proceedings from the gold-medallist's 'perch'. I have always regretted not having a return match with Dick, as I would have liked to try and square the series

was going to be short-lived, then the end would not be an ig-
nominious one.

We reckoned that Black's 55·5 seconds 110 yards short-
course record was worth 55·2 seconds for metres, plus a maximum of 1·4 seconds for his extra two turns, giving a probable
long-course metric time of about 56·6 seconds, or about 0·5
seconds slower than my effort in Germany. But two factors
impossible to reckon were in Black's favour. The first was that
on his record swim he had had no competition, and the second
was his well-known liking for long-course swimming. However
one worked it out, it seemed clear that a first-class race was in
the offing.

As I had given my all in Germany, I could not really expect
any improvement in the six days between the two swims. It
would have been pointless to pile on a great deal of extra training, as this would only have had the immediate effect of sapping the body's reserves of strength and I would probably have
swum slower. My father always worked on the principle of
having me fresh and well-rested for big events, and so we spent
the few intervening days on fast sprint work, with plenty of
rests. He also made quite sure that I was in a very positive, confident frame of mind, and did I find a use for that!

'Come in. Sit down. I hope you didn't get too used to being
first last weekend, because you'll be second tomorrow.' Those
were just about the first words that Ian Black ever spoke to me.
It was the Friday before the match with West Germany and I
had just joined Black in his compartment on the Blackpool
train at Glasgow Central station. I had expected to find a
highly-competitive personality, but this was ridiculous! We
were the only Scots in the team and the only two travellers in
the compartment, so our comments to one another were not in
any way inhibited by the presence of outsiders. This was just
as well for me, because I was far too self-conscious to have
engaged in the kind of verbal warfare which followed, if anyone else had been present. Black on the other hand gave the
impression of being totally oblivious to anything but our im-

D

pending confrontation and throughout the entire journey I was bombarded by a constant stream of facts and figures, all of which made a Black victory inevitable. I was fast, that he granted me, but I lacked the stamina and distance work which real long-course sprinters had to have. He would 'do a Konrads' on me, referring to the victory in the Australian championship of the great middle- and long-distance swimmer, Jon Konrads, who had surprisingly come from behind in the closing stages of the 110 yards sprint as the established 'pure' sprinters were fading.

But for the careful mental preparation which my father had instilled into me, I might well have crumpled under the onslaught, but I did not. In fact I was surprised at the relish with which I bounded into the fray. 'No, you won't take me from behind, because I'll be too far ahead for that. You know I am a good second faster than you over fifty yards (a fact I knew he couldn't deny). Well, I can hold that pace for three-quarters of the race, if I wish, and even you cannot take three yards off me in twenty-five yards.'

And so it went on, not only for the train journey, but after our arrival at Blackpool, at the hotel, at the evening training session in the pool and at the breakfast table. The rest of the team were on my side, but nobody openly challenged Black's behaviour, such was his eminence in British swimming. He had been the undisputed king since 1958, and although he had temporarily abdicated in 1961, his early-season performances in 1962 had firmly reinstated him on his throne. The British swimming team was his court, and no coach, official or swimmer willingly incurred his displeasure.

So this was the man who had done so much for British swimming? This was the man whom I had so admired and who had inspired me to reach out for the highest prizes in swimming. I made a firm resolve then, that if ever I had any great success the man whose behaviour I least wanted to emulate was Ian Black.

Although I was more than a little sick at heart at the open

hostility into which our relationship seemed to have developed, I steeled myself for the race with a passion such as I had never before experienced. Never had I detested an opponent as I now did. I wanted to win or die in the attempt.

The race when it came was something of an anti-climax, for Black was never in the hunt and he finished third in the poor time of 57·8 seconds, 1·3 seconds behind my winning effort. Immediately after the race the unpredictable Black was the first to congratulate me, and he was lavish in his statements to the Press – 'No excuses from me. Bobby was magnificent.'

I found his attitude in defeat totally incomprehensible, for he behaved like an English gentleman cricketer of the old school. He was a paragon of good sportsmanship and as such completely took the wind out of my sails. I had taken an almost sadistic delight in defeating him and had frankly looked forward to watching him squirm afterwards. But the bitter instinct which he had bred in me faded within minutes of the race ending in the face of his chameleon-like charm. I found myself talking about Black to the Press in a manner which shortly before would have demanded the persuasion of a fiendish Chinese torture – 'I've always dreamed of swimming alongside Ian Black. It was my greatest ambition to be in the British team with him. I'm not fooled by his lapse tonight. He's still capable of great things.'

After the gala, as I walked quite alone and muttering to myself, along the windswept promenade, I tried to make sense of Black's behaviour. Was his pre-race treatment of me uncharacteristic and merely the result of a temporarily troubled personality? Or had I been manipulated by him before and after the race and been given my first real lesson in public relations? Neither then nor since have I found an acceptable answer to these questions, nor have I managed to form a satisfactory impression of Black's true character. The day after the sprint, he was beaten in his favourite 440 yards event, in a time fourteen seconds below his best, and immediately afterwards he announced his retirement.

We met several times in later years and always he was

friendliness and politeness personified. He sent me a telegram of congratulations when I broke my first world record, and a telegram and letter when I won the silver medal in Tokyo.

He was obviously a sportsman who relied tremendously on a 'killer' instinct and I believe that it ran amok at the time of our first confrontation simply because, as I discovered later, he was very unfit for the match (due to swotting for his university finals) and should never have agreed to compete.

It was also said to me by a friend who knew Black intimately, that he went to the West German match specifically to commit sporting suicide. Black knew that in his unfit condition he could not beat either myself or the West German star, Gerhard Hetz, but he wanted a public excuse for stepping off the treadmill of training, which he had driven harder than any British swimmer before or since.

It seems a strange theory, but then Black seemed a strange person, although it is now my opinion, reinforced by my sub-sequent acquaintance with him, that he was basically of a shy nature. This shyness, I believe, sometimes turned to aggression only as a result of the overwhelming publicity he received while still in his teens. I doubt if any young personality could have remained unaffected. Whatever the reasons for his often puzzling behaviour, it is one of my greatest regrets that he did not con-tinue to compete at his best in my era. The results for both of us and for Britain might have been startling.

VII. The Big Circuit

They say that the more one learns, the more one realizes how much remains to be learnt. Well, so it was also with my swimming progress. There I was in June 1962, just turned eighteen, undisputed king-pin of British swimming, but only beginning to appreciate fully the enormity of the task I had set myself in aiming for a gold medal in Tokyo two years later. My best time of 56·1 seconds was still 2·5 seconds outside the world record of the Brazilian, Dos Santos, and I knew that the world's leading sprinters would probably be even faster than that by 1964. Both my father and I thought I was capable of improving more than a second a year, but only if the training load was increased and I had regular top-class competition. The latter requirement would certainly be fulfilled in 1962 with the European championships in Leipzig in August and the Commonwealth Games in Australia in November, and with the long college holidays from June to October we hoped also to step up my training to a level more in keeping with other swimmers of my class around the world.

Immediately after my two international victories in June, therefore, I embarked on a greatly increased training programme with the idea of training through any competitions which took place in the two months before the championships at Leipzig. This meant that I could not be in peak sprinting condition throughout July, but it was a procedure which my father and I were always to follow, for we discovered comparatively early in my career that I needed to 'peak' for an event, and this demanded a fairly long 'tapering' off of training. Our plan was, therefore, a simple one. We aimed for peak condition for the last two weeks of August, which would take in the A.S.A. championships and the European Games, then a slight easing off for the first two weeks in September, and a second build-up through late September and October for the Commonwealth Games in November.

It says a great deal for my father's foresight as a coach that he organized my training in this manner, because many British swimmers and coaches year after year make the mistake of trying to maintain peak form for the whole of the impossibly long British season from April to October. Selecting my major targets in this manner made it much easier for me to be sure of good swims when I most needed them.

This training strategy for the summer of 1962 also gives an illustration of the rapidly-developed confidence which we both now had in my ability to stay at the top in Britain. The trials for the European Games were in late July and yet we intended making no special effort to peak for them properly.

At the beginning of July Britain had another away match, this time with Hungary in Budapest. I approached this trip with decidedly mixed feelings. The Hungarians had an excellent record in European and even world swimming, and I was particularly interested in seeing the conditions their sportsmen enjoyed at home. My keenness was severely curtailed, however, by the knowledge that I had not been doing the kind of training conducive to optimum sprint performances, and I sensed that even my best might not be good enough for at least one of the Hungarians.

Having already visited one Communist country I frankly expected the second to be similar, but my preconceived ideas of Hungary were wildly inaccurate. The difference could be summed up in two words – colour and smiles. The twin cities of Buda and Pest seemed incredibly beautiful to my budding architectural appreciation and the people also appeared a great deal happier and less stereotyped in dress than in East Germany.

These factors, together with gloriously sunny weather, gave our stay a distinct holiday flavour, which was spoiled by the rather poor swimming of our men, who could muster only one victory. The British girls won most of their events, but the match overall went to the Hungarians.

I had my first bitter taste of world-class sprinting and could finish only third in 57·5 seconds behind the two Magyars. The winner was Gyula Dobai, who had been fifth in the Rome Olympics, and his time of 55·7 seconds was one of the fastest in Europe that year. In retrospect, I think it was fortunate that I had not peaked for this swim, for it is unlikely that I could have beaten Dobai on that occasion, no matter what my condition. He was in magnificent shape and had a great psychological boost in being cheered home by the largest crowd I had ever seen at a swimming match. In the circumstances, I attributed my poorish performance entirely to the type of training I had been intentionally carrying out at home, and so I left St Margaret's Island in the middle of the Danube with my confidence comparatively unscathed. Indeed, I found myself looking forward to the European Games even more keenly, when I hoped to square matters with both the Hungarian sprinters.

Stan Clarke again contrived to carve himself a permanent niche in my memory through his 'extra curricular' activities. He insisted on carrying out a ridiculous 'dare' during a sight-seeing tour and performed a hand-stand on the battlements of Budapest Castle, where the slightest mistake would have resulted in a sheer drop of about two hundred feet to the rocks below. He was afterwards much more perturbed at losing a cheap ball-point pen, which he had forgotten to remove from his pocket, than he was by our white-faced denunciation of his foolhardiness.

Shortly after my return from Budapest I won the British trial at Blackpool in 57·1 seconds, and my confident speculation about gaining a place in the team for Leipzig became fact. It only remained for me to show that the McGregor method of preparing for my first truly international event was the correct one.

Although still only half-way through its full course, the 1962 season had been already an extremely eventful and successful one for me. It had taught me a great deal in a relatively short space of time, and I had been a willing pupil. As a result of this high-pressure introduction into the international sports arena, it was in many respects a quite different Bobby McGregor who stood poised for his first European Games in August compared to the tentative and somewhat naïve schoolboy who had won his first British cap only three months earlier. I had learnt a great deal about the business of international swimming, but the greatest changes had occurred in my awareness of the niceties of social behaviour. It is not that I was a boor or an idiot beforehand, but the average product of a modest home and the State school system has little experience of the world outside his own immediate social and geographical environment, and when he first crosses these boundaries the effect on his general character can be striking.

I was rapidly becoming much more confident and much more careful about my appearance, for I now realized that I had a position to maintain and I wanted my image to be a good one. Reporters no longer terrified me and I remember overhearing one Fleet Street man commenting to a colleague just after he had interviewed me – 'In May I could hardly get him to tell me his name and now it's "Just call me if you want to know anything, folks".'

The Press, however, marvellous though they had been to me up till then, presented one of the three new problems which I had to face at the European Games. In the numerous previews of the championships, I was almost unanimously tipped for a medal of some kind in the 100 metres freestyle. This was, of course, perfectly justifiable journalism, for, as an improving swimmer who had done good times all summer, my fifth place in the European ranking lists was a genuine basis for speculating on my medal chances. But pleasant though it was to be described in flattering terms in print, it had the additional effect of making me realize that people throughout the country might *expect* me to win a medal and therefore be disappointed and possibly consider me a failure if I finished out of the first three.

This problem dogged me throughout much of my career, although I became better equipped to deal with it in later years. On that first occasion, however, it was an unsettling addition to my more obvious anxieties.

The second problem was the length of our stay in Leipzig. I had never spent more than a few days away from the watchful eyes of my father, and although he had always stressed to me the importance of my being able to train on my own and make my own decisions, nevertheless I knew that this very important event was to be the acid test of how much of his instructions I had managed to take in.

The third problem was also a new one in that I would be required to do heats and a semi-final on the opening day of the competitions, with the final the following day. And if, as expected, the men's medley and freestyle teams also reached the finals, I would have seven major efforts in seven days! This is the kind of programme that an Ian Black, with his massive training loads and great stamina, would have revelled in, but to me, the pure sprinter with relatively little mileage behind me, it presented a terrifying prospect.

The European Championships at Leipzig did indeed provide the first comprehensive test of my resilience to the complex demands of top-flight international sport, and I think I probably passed with flying colours.

Although I finished only fourth in the individual 100 metres freestyle, I had won my heat and semi-final with improving swims, and my time of 55·7 seconds in the final was a personal best performance. The three medal winners were all much more experienced than myself, yet the result showed that I had not been outclassed: Alain Gottvalles (France) 55·2 seconds, Per Lindberg (Sweden) 55·5 seconds and Ronnie Kroon (Holland) 55·5 seconds.

I was very pleased with myself and not the least bit disappointed that I had not won a medal. I knew that the manner in which I had continued to improve made it inevitable that these tangible trappings of success would eventually come my way and my father had always made me aware of the dangers of expecting too much too soon.

But the victory ceremony itself made a powerful impression on me. The race had finished only minutes before and I was making my way through the crowded stands to the position near the top where the British team always gathered. I had still some way to go when the spectators surrounding me began to stand, so I too stopped and watched as the three flags were slowly pulled to the top of their poles and 'La Marseillaise' rang round the stadium. My eyes riveted themselves on Gotvalles's gold medal which stood out against the Frenchman's blue track suit, and reflected the late afternoon sun. Moist-eyed I continued my climb, knowing that I would not rest until I too had brought an audience to its feet in a show of respect for my flag and my anthem.

We had a fine spirit at these Games, greatly helped by the commanding presence of Bert Kinnear, the team coach, and after the individual sprint was over at the beginning of the week-long programme, all the sprinters focussed their attention on to the men's 4 × 100 metres freestyle team race, in which we knew we had a great chance of a gold medal.

The final of that event is memorable for two quite unrelated reasons. The first was my own performance of 54·1 seconds on the last leg, which was the fastest 100 metres of the entire championships. I went in third behind Lindberg and Gottvalles, passed the Swede in the final twenty metres and touched home for the silver, just one second behind the Frenchman.

When our split times were announced we saw that one of our team had dropped two seconds compared with his time in the individual event. We all knew that he had spent most of the previous night in the bed of a particularly attractive Danish blonde and to us the chemical formula of that particular situation was very simple! In the changing-room the two other relay men and myself approached our miserable team mate, making it quite plain that we intended to wring his neck with the ribbon of the silver medal which still hung there. 'Honest, fellas,' he shouted as we grabbed him, 'the only reason I did it was 'cos I'd spent the night before my individual race wiv 'er, and I did my best time then!'

The apparent unassailability of this logic saved him from a good-natured beating-up, but I remember thinking to myself that here was surely confirmation that sex was far too volatile an ingredient to be allowed in the life of an athlete in training.

Two weeks later I won my first A.S.A. title at Blackpool with a further improvement to 55·6 seconds for the 110 yards. It was expected that I would win, so I experienced no great pleasure when I confirmed the form-book, indeed my only memory is one of disappointment at failing to improve Ian Black's British record of 55·5 seconds. However, the ramifications of my swim were important, for I was now the top-ranked sprinter in the Commonwealth, and therefore favourite for the gold medal at Perth in November.

I had been looking forward to competing against the reigning Olympic Champion, John Devitt, but as he had announced his retirement, I decided to try for the next best thing at Perth, his world record of 55·2 seconds. My father thought I was capable of it, so, after a brief respite towards the end of September, we trained harder than ever throughout October before I finally set off at the beginning of November.

The Commonwealth Games are quite different from any other big international sports festival. It is not an exaggeration to call them a family affair, because this is exactly the impression one has and I found myself immediately caught up in the sunshine and happy, holiday atmosphere.

The Scottish swimming team had no coach, due to lack of funds, so we were left to our own devices as far as training was concerned. I tried to train hard, but our situation out there provided at one and the same time every conceivable facility for perfect training and every most desirable distraction!

The accommodation in the Games Village consisted of a colony of new luxury houses, each of which housed a few competitors in a self-contained 'family' unit. There was a magnificent palm-fringed beach only 400 yards from our quarters and this proved a much more attractive lure than the fifty-metre training-pool which was also sited in close proximity to the village. The days were spent in forcing oneself to do some training before making straight for the beach where we tried to master the art of surfing on the great Malibu boards. The nights found us still on the sands, singing and enjoying barbecues round huge wood fires before drifting off on to the dunes with a couple of blankets and the partner of our choice. I read recently that an English table-tennis player reckoned he had been dropped from the team because he was found holding hands with another competitor. By those criteria there would have been several dawn executions in Perth!

Looking back I now realize that with the exception of the restaurant, the accommodation in the village was virtually unnecessary.

The constant tug-of-war between myself and my conscience ended in a points victory for self-indulgence, which was perhaps pardonable in an eighteen-year-old, but as in all such cases, retribution was swift and painful.

I won my heat of the 110 yards freestyle in a new Games record of 55·8 seconds, and was the fastest qualifier for the final. I could not repeat this performance, however, and the gold medal went to Dick Pound of Canada in the same time of 55·8 seconds with myself second in 56·1 seconds.

I was naturally disappointed but I had learnt an important lesson; that it is the whole person who stands on the block, not just the part which has done the training. I believe I had the ability to win that race and would have done so but for spending too much time sunbathing, surfing and party-going. I was not prodigal in this respect, indeed I was a saint in comparison with some competitors, but I enjoyed myself enough to halt temporarily the improving graph of my swimming performance. Dick Pound, on the other hand, fully deserved his victory because he had prepared himself in such a way that the best performance of his career came at just the right time.

During this trip I had the pleasure of meeting Dawn Fraser and Murray Rose, two superb Australian swimmers who had already assured themselves of a permanent place among the élite of world sport. I became friendly with both of them and as an impressionable newcomer to the front rank of international sport it was just as well that I met Murray at the same time as Dawn, otherwise I might well have been swept off my feet by the infectious exuberance of the fun-loving Australian girl, who by winning the women's sprint in three successive Olympic Games proved herself the greatest female swimmer of this or any other era.

Dawn and her pal, Linda McGill, were leading lights in many carefree escapades in which I was a willing participant away from the competition pool. Their dislike of the dictates of officialdom was apparent even then, and it came as no surprise to me two years later when they were both banned from competing for Australia after alleged misdemeanours at the Tokyo Olympics. I met Linda in England in 1965 after she had turned professional and I was highly amused to learn from her that she intended to become the first swimmer to conquer the Channel – in the nude! At the last moment, however, the Channel Swimming Association insisted that she wear a regulation outfit. She successfully negotiated the trip in spite of being a little disgusted that a new kind of officialdom had thwarted yet another typical McGill project. The incident received considerable press coverage and I am sure most people saw it as a publicity gimmick, but knowing Linda as I do I have no doubt at all that she meant it.

Murray Rose, on the other hand, was as responsible as the girls were frivolous and his behaviour in Perth and on the many occasions I met him afterwards in various parts of the world always made him appear the perfect example of a sporting ambassador. He was friendly, approachable and extremely helpful even on our first meeting, and although not in the least straightlaced he nevertheless seemed to know where to draw the line of moderation in most things. He had adjusted remarkably well to the constant attention which prowess at sport, particularly in swimming, can impose upon a youthful, developing personality. I unashamedly decided to try to model my behaviour on his and I was delighted that we became and have remained good friends ever since.

From my many happy memories of that marvellous month in Australia, one incident stands out as being typical of the uninhibited atmosphere of these 'Family Games'. It had little to do with international sports, although it received a bigger ovation than many a Gold-medal-winning effort.

On the outskirts of Perth there was a new open-air swimming-pool, which quickly became a favourite recreational and sunbathing spot for the Games competitors and for many of the young ladies of the city. The changing-rooms had not been completed in time for the Games opening and it had been decided to postpone further building until most of the Games visitors had departed. Swimmers and sunbathers had therefore to undress in wooden huts which were separated from the pool by about fifty yards of rough, stony ground.

During a fun game of water-polo one of the swimmers' trunks were accidentally ripped off and then intentionally thrown from the pool. His demands for their return only added to the general amusement and eventually he was resigned to remaining in the water until the crowd dispersed or until someone took pity on him and threw him a pair of trunks.

But his sadistic colleagues were far from finished. He was dragged from the water. He took refuge, face down in a six-inch-deep, three-feet-wide footbath which surrounded the pool, and lay there while everybody enjoyed the joke. After a short time, and to thunderous applause, he stood up and sprinted for the hut, which he reached in double-quick time, in spite of giving a fair imitation of the Highland Fling en route, as the many small stones hurt his feet!

After four weeks and a half of luxurious leisure in the Australian sun my homecoming on 9 December was for once a little reluctant, principally because I was now more than a month behind in my studies at the Glasgow College of Architecture, and I knew I would have to work very hard to catch up. Nevertheless, the year ended on a high note, for I was named Scottish Sportsman of the Year in December, and on Hogmanay, as the Old Year was fading, my father and I drank a toast to a joint resolution that I would break the world record for the 110 yards freestyle during the following season.

VIII. Life at the Top

Whether our toast had anything to do with it or not, 1963 certainly turned out to be a very successful year, during which I was spurred on by the knowledge that the matches arranged for that season offered me the opportunity of meeting most of the men who had bested me in 1962. The main aim of competitive sport must be the man-to-man encounter and I was never happy unless I could avenge a previous defeat.

Before the season was properly under way, however, I was invited to compete in Iceland for ten days along with fellow Scottish champions Ann Baxter and Andy Harrower.

We arrived very late one cold black winter's night and as we sped through the snows between the airport and Reyjkavick our first impressions of the country were anything but favourable. We eventually arrived at a beautiful luxury hotel, but even its princely comfort did little to cheer me up, for I was already beginning to dread the ensuing days in what appeared to be a dismal, dreary outpost of civilization. I retired immediately and enjoyed my usual deep sleep.

I awoke fairly early the next morning and amused myself in the first moments of consciousness by exploring the functions of several buttons which figured on a bedside console. Suddenly the curtains gently swished open to reveal a complete wall of glass and beyond that the most spectacular view I have ever experienced. My room was in the penthouse of the hotel and I found myself looking down on the whole of Reyjkavick, which lay glistening white in the sunshine between a pale blue cloudless sky and the steel blue glassy sea. It was breathtaking. My initial misgivings about Iceland disappeared in an instant and I went on to enjoy one of my most interesting trips ever.

The solitary swimming gala took place the same day and we were pleased to win all the events in which we swam. The Icelanders seemed delighted also that we had set their swimmers new standards to aim for and they afterwards overwhelmed us with such kindness that our visit was truly memorable.

We enjoyed the unusually invigorating experience of bathing out of doors in the natural hot springs, then rolling in the February snows, and I also indulged with considerable success in my particular passion for fishing. But the most unforgettable aspect of the visit was the never-ending party-going which seems to be the only social diversion in the Far North.

The Icelanders, together with the Russians, are the most heartily hospitable people I have ever met, and we soon found that it was impossible not to join them in a few convivial drinks. Being Scottish we were inevitably plied with fearsome tots of our national drink at our 'going-away' party, which was held in the beautiful home of our host, a man of great wealth, whose exquisite taste was clearly reflected in the profusion of fine works of art with which we were surrounded. As the evening wore on I grew drowsy with dancing so much and, feeling the backs of my knees touch against a hard edge, I assumed it was a chair and sat down. The table (as it turned out to be) disintegrated and I found myself sitting not so much among a pile of recognizable wooden splinters as among a heap of fine wood dust! The hush which descended on the company confirmed what I already suspected; that the table was an extremely old and valuable antique.

I sat there stunned, in abject embarrassment, until my host helped me to my feet with the reassuring comment that it was 'not an important piece'. But the manner in which he had steeled himself by quickly downing a near tumbler full of the hard stuff before approaching me gave the lie to his immaculate manners.

E

Many times subsequently I have involuntarily blushed on remembering this incident and I discovered, as the result of a remarkable coincidence, that my host had not forgotten it either. More than five years later I was window-shopping in the most expensive part of Mexico City soon after my arrival there, when my eyes met those of my Icelandic friend, who was inside one shop. He immediately came out his face covered in smiles and after greeting me warmly said: 'I am thinking of buying one of these for your next visit!' indicating one of the low, bronze-legged onyx tables which the shop specialized in! There were obviously no hard feelings, however, for that evening I was treated to an excellent dinner, as he picked my brains about the swimming events, which he had travelled so far to see.

After my return from Iceland, I trained hard for the opening of the international season in June, when a Scottish and Welsh select was competing in a triangular match with England and France at Perth. This was much more than just another international match, for I realized that the European champion and record holder, Alain Gottvalles, might turn out for the French and I desperately wanted to meet him now that I was much more experienced than at Leipzig the previous year. I was kept on tenterhooks until the French team actually arrived in Scotland, when it was confirmed that Gotvalles was their sprint selection.

As the Frenchmen had travelled straight from the Côte d'Azur, where they had been involved in initial team training for the Tokyo Olympics, it was expected that they would produce some outstanding swimming, but they were extremely disappointing and were thrashed by England, and only narrowly defeated the Scotland/Wales selection.

Gottvalles was particularly unimpressive and was never in the hunt in the 110 yards freestyle. I led from start to finish and won by the very impressive margin of 1·8 seconds in a new British record time of 55·2 seconds. I was particularly pleased at having reduced Ian Black's record by ·3 of a second, and although this was a short-course match, my time of 55·2 seconds was obviously within striking distance of the European long-course metric record (55·0 seconds) and the world's linear record (55·1) of John Devitt.

Two weeks later, at the fast salt-water twenty-five-yard pool in Dundee, I served notice of the likelihood of my being among the 'big' records before the season was over, when I swam an official 110-yard record attempt at 53·4 seconds. This broke every record in the book from the world 100 metres down to the Scottish Native, but because of the additional turns in the small pool, I could only claim national and not international records. Nevertheless, I knew then that I was in superb condition and I could barely wait for my first long-course competition the following month when Britain was to meet Sweden at the Derby baths in Blackpool.

This match saw the realization of two of my targets. I defeated the Leipzig silver medallist Per Ola Lindberg and my time of 54·4 was a new world 110-yard and European 100-metre record. My delight was enhanced by the fact that I had surprisingly been made team captain just before the match and I felt I had thanked the team manager, John Zimmerman, in the most appropriate manner.

Among the many telegrams I received on the second day of the meeting was one from the Olympic Gold Medallist of 1960, John Devitt, whose world record I had just beaten. It read as follows: 'Congratulations! It's the greatest record in the book. Be proud of it. Make up the double at Tokyo.'

His sporting words gave me a great fillip and I almost felt sorry for depriving him of his record! But they had the added effect of making me determined to emulate his even greater achievement at the Olympic Games, and to be as gracious myself some day to another emerging champion. Beneath the pleasure of achieving some of my major ambitions, however, lay an even deeper feeling of satisfaction, that a decision taken entirely by myself, and which at the time had seemed risky, had been vindicated.

My training loads for this match had seldom dropped below 5,000 yards a day – all of it hard swimming – and three weeks before the meeting I thought I felt myself going 'over the top', or stale. The rest of the family was holidaying in a remote croft at the Gairloch, in the extreme north-west of Scotland, so I took off from Falkirk and joined them for two weeks of rest and recreational sea swimming. I returned to Falkirk completely refreshed, did a few days very light water work, then set out for Blackpool. My performance there endorsed the decision to stop training and this showed me that I was beginning to understand myself and think for myself, which in many ways is more important than world records.

The change that this one swim made on my life was well summed up by one of the sports writers of the time – 'but although he had his own way in the water, this student of Glasgow's College of Architecture must now accept the responsibility, the glamour and the attentions he has earned with this one shattering swim'. I was now a real national (i.e. British) sports personality, and whereas in the past my scrapbook had been filled mainly with clippings from the Scottish newspapers, now the London dailies, and the well-known London writers were beginning to give me star treatment, which, in fact, I was delighted to accept!

The battle was far from won, however, and Lindberg and Gottvalles promptly showed that on their own ground they could still be formidable opponents. The Swede set a new European 100-metre record of 54·3 seconds in a time trial in Sweden, but was then defeated in an international event in France, when Gottvalles swam home in 54·6 seconds.

The A.S.A. championships in August offered me the first opportunity of replying to these distant challenges. I had grown to like the Derby baths enormously and was looking forward to the final-night atmosphere which always seemed to be worth a few tenths of a second to me. But on this occasion my eager anticipation was clouded by a new problem which made life very difficult for me in the few days before the sprint final, and which was to present a permanent temptation for the rest of my swimming career – the attentions of hero-worshipping girls.

I have always had a healthy appreciation of the opposite sex, suitably balanced by judicious restraint, but from the summer of 1963 onwards the delicate equilibrium of these matters was in constant jeopardy. In practice it usually meant that a couple of girls would be 'in attendance' wherever I went, making it quite clear that they were available. I soon became oblivious to their presence when I was in public with many of my own friends around, but occasionally the more daring of them would engage in quite frightening clandestine activities.

I returned to my sea-front boarding-house one night and made straight for my bedroom. I switched on the light and found a female head shyly protruding above the bed-cover. I had never set eyes on the girl before and on confirming that it really was my own room, I asked her what she was doing there. Her answer was to pull down the cover and expose her nude bosom!

'Get dressed and get out,' I shouted, as I beat a hasty retreat and sought out a girl swimmer whom I knew well and who was also a guest at the house. Together we returned to my room, where the over-zealous intruder had by now accepted my lack of interest and was already fully dressed. As she left the room she turned towards me and kissed me on the cheek, before finally disappearing along the corridor.

I was considerably perturbed by the incident. Although the girl in question looked sixteen or seventeen, she could well have been less, and she was certainly of an age and character which suggested that she would enjoy talking about her 'experience' to her friends. It worried me that her version of what had happened might not be strictly accurate, for I had no wish to become known as a sporting Romeo. I myself kept very quiet about the episode and never forgot to lock my room thereafter.

It would be wrong, however, to imagine that it was only immature adolescents who could be so blatantly enticing in their behaviour. On a subsequent occasion, while a guest at an Embassy cocktail party, I found myself making the usual small-talk with the wives of two diplomatic officials. One of the ladies left and she was barely out of earshot when the other, a beautiful elegant woman in her mid-thirties, dramatically switched the direction of our conversation.

'When you walk into a room I am sure all the women find themselves irresistibly drawn to you – as I do.' The line was delivered with an aplomb completely in keeping with her sophisticated appearance and I felt myself straining to maintain an equally unruffled pose as I unsuccessfully tried to think of a suitably matter-of-fact reply. Before I could answer, however, she had gone on to invite me to her apartment, ostensibly so that she 'could show me over the city', but the manner in which her eyes took me in from head to toe and the comments that her husband would be away for a few days, left me in no doubt as to the underlying motivation for her offer. I excused myself on the grounds of team training and beat a hasty and appropriately diplomatic, albeit embarrassed, retreat.

Only recently this anecdote from the past contributed to my huge enjoyment of the film 'The Graduate', in which a young man of about my own age finds himself in a similar situation.

Such external matters, although unsettling at the time, were always eliminated from my mind when the moment of competition arrived, and so it was with unimpaired confidence that I set about retaining my A.S.A. title. On the Saturday evening the waters and atmosphere of the Derby baths again turned up trumps for me, for I improved my world record by 0·3 seconds with a swim of 54·1 seconds, which also, of course, regained the European metric record.

European sprinting had reached an unprecendented peak, and even the Americans could not significantly better our per-formances, which served as a magnificent publicity build-up for the Six Nations match at Blackpool in September, when Europe's leading sprinters would be representing their respective countries.

Originally I had been very keen to compete during September in the World Student Games in Brazil. I had always been fascinated by South America and it would have been doubly exhilarating to spend a few weeks there and perhaps also satisfy another ambition of winning a gold medal. The British selectors, however, had stressed the importance of fielding their strongest team for the Six Nations match, which was being held in Britain for the first time, and I therefore decided to forgo the unknown splendours of Rio de Janeiro for the familiar pleasures of the Golden Mile.

For once the British Press offered a comprehensive preview coverage of a swimming event in the days before it actually took place and this generated tremendous interest in the meeting, which was relayed to more than 100 million televiewers throughout Western Europe.

This match saw the opening of a five-year-long cold war between myself and the French Pressmen, who were without question the most partisan sports writers I ever met. On this occasion they were clearly trying to rattle me, and two French reporters badgered me to state whether I would beat Gottvalles, who it seemed, was in scintillating form. I replied that I was confident of defeating him then and at any time in the foreseeable future. Such comments were not typical of me, for although I tried to *think* like this before my races, I detested braggarts and I usually made an effort to be generous to my opponents and avoided provocative remarks. I don't think Gottvalles ever spoke to me again after that, although we had several subsequent conversations by proxy through the medium of the French sporting Press!

The race itself provided a fitting climax to a great meeting for Britain. We won the match and I set new world and European figures with a 54·0 seconds swim, a full second faster than Gotvalles, who was followed home by Lindberg and Kroon.

The most pleasing feature of my swim was that the equivalent time for 100 metres would have been about 53·6 seconds, which was the current world record of the Brazilian Dos Santos. Generally speaking the world's metric records were vastly superior to the comparable linear distances, simply because all other countries competed mainly over metres and these distances were therefore under the greatest and most consistent international pressure. British swimmers had often received disproportionate publicity for breaking world records over yards distances with performances which were greatly inferior to the equivalent metric records usually considered to be the 'real' world records. After my Six Nations swim I was untroubled when I saw myself described as the 'fastest swimmer in the world', for I now felt I had earned the title, particularly as the Dos Santos swim was considered 'suspect'. It had been done in a solo time-trial, during which the Brazilian had stopped and started again after being dissatisfied with his initial turn.

I finished the season as the world's top-ranked swimmer over 100 metres and that, with the consistency I had shown, made it inevitable that there would be widespread speculation about my chances of an Olympic gold medal. One writer was prompted to describe me as the 'winter ante-post favourite' for the Olympic title. His form assessment was right, of course, but the continuing prosperity of bookmakers emphasized to me the high casualty rate of favourites, and racehorses were spared one of the major problems of any high-pressure event – they couldn't read!

IX. Striking for Gold

Living through an Olympic year is a difficult experience for anyone who has aspirations to take part in the Games, but for those who are the acknowledged favourites for certain events, it becomes an ordeal. One is constantly aware that many years' work has to be concentrated at the right time for what is almost certainly a never-to-be repeated tilt at the ultimate accolade in sport. Yet sheer luck can play a major role in deciding the victor and vanquished, particularly in the short events, where fractions of a second assume a quite disproportionate importance.

Even the year in which the Games take place can be lucky for some and not so lucky for others. Four years is a long time in any sportsman's life and it has often happened that an athlete has reached his peak in the year after one Olympic Games and been the world's acknowledged champion for the next three years before deteriorating as the next Games took place.

I was fortunate in this latter respect, because the Olympics had fallen particularly well for me and I therefore approached them with no thoughts of a second attempt. I knew that this was my biggest challenge and I intended to rise to it decisively.

The months before went well. I had opened my season in April with a good victory in the Great Britain v. U.S.S.R. match, only 0·1 seconds slower than my own world record. In May I equalled the record in the match against Holland, and then eased down in training till the beginning of July, when I began the massive build-up for the A.S.A. championships and Olympic Trials at the beginning of September.

73

I was receiving tremendous publicity throughout the year as 'Britain's leading gold medal hope in any sport', and although I was grateful that the writers, and, therefore, the public, were taking a great interest in myself and in swimming, I would have preferred them to play down my chances. Apart from that, however, I was in excellent physical, psychological and even academic shape for I had taken no time off from university in order to train and I managed to pass all my exams.

I had also succeeded in carrying out virtually to the letter the demanding programme of training which my father and I had carefully prepared and initiated the previous November. I had also been untroubled by illness. Indeed, so well balanced and confident was I throughout the summer months, that I was quite unperturbed when Gottvalles beat the world's 100-metre record with an excellent 52·9 seconds swim in Hungary.

To be frank, the time was faster than I thought I would probably achieve in Tokyo, but I felt sure in my bones that neither Gottvalles nor anyone else would go that fast under the pressure of the Olympic final. It came as no surprise to me when I learned later that the Frenchman had done it as the first swimmer of their relay squad in an international match against Hungary, a situation which breeds much less competitive tension than an individual event.

My own best pre-Olympic swim was in winning the A.S.A. title when I again broke my world's 110-yard record with a time of 53·9 seconds, which would have given me a metric equivalent of about 53·5 seconds, after allowing the usual 0·4-second differentiation from yards to metres.

Although I had never aimed at a particular target time for Tokyo, preferring to work on the principle that the sky is the limit, I had nevertheless always believed that 53·5 seconds would probably win the gold, and considerable weight was lent to my opinion when the American Olympic trial results became known: Ilman 53·8, Schollander 53·9 and Austin 54·1 (53·7 in heat). These were the men I considered to be my main rivals in Tokyo, in spite of Gotvalles's world record.

I was delighted to be made captain of the British team, which was under the direction of Bert Kinnear as coach and Alf Price as team manager, and a happy team it proved to be.

Team spirit is a grand-sounding expression which one hears a great deal in sporting circles, but its meaning in practice is usually vastly different from what the outsider expects. The 1964 team displayed all the most attractive features of team spirit in the best sense, with a completely unselfish dedication by every individual to the well-being of the whole team. This was a team where the words 'All the best' meant what they say and not 'Don't do any better than I'm going to do', which is the attitude that undermines many teams, and is particularly rife among sportswomen.

The training which the team carried out together in the National Recreation Centre at Crystal Palace was the hardest any of us had ever undertaken. We were together for ten days, during which we averaged three to four training sessions a day, and everybody went through hell. But, as so often happens when a group of individuals suffers together, the common agony fuses them into a single unit and a real sympathy for one another springs up.

This very demanding training continued until a week before the Games, at which point everyone in the team was swimming faster than ever before. At this stage, Kinnear, excellent coach and leader that he was, made in my opinion the only mistake of his entire team preparation; he began an over-long and abrupt training 'taper' for the whole team.

His reasoning was understandable and logical. No team under his supervision had ever absorbed so much work in such a short space of time. He had already achieved spectacular success, as shown by the training performances of everybody in the squad, and he therefore thought that a longer pre-competition rest would be beneficial. Unfortunately it did not work out that way, for most of the team had slumped considerably by the time they came to compete and in many cases their times in the

Olympic events were actually slower than they had been doing in repetition swims in training only two weeks earlier.

After three or four days of doing little training, I felt myself 'falling off the peak' and I actually recommenced fairly hard work in the days immediately before my races. I still did not feel absolutely right during my heat and semi-final swims, but I did feel perfectly poised for the final.

I certainly was confident before that final. Only Gottvalles had ever swum faster than myself and having beaten him comfortably in our last two encounters I felt I could do so again.

My position *vis-à-vis* Gottvalles was helped immensely by the French Press. Whereas the British Press has a tendency to be over-critical of a star who may not have performed up to standard, the French will search out every conceivable excuse for the defeat of one of their 'vedettes'.

It may be as a result of this that the French have never struck me as being great competitors. I can think of many of their swimmers, and some athletes too, who were marvellous against the clock, but who consistently failed against the man. They seem to be so pampered and adulated at home that, like spoiled children, they can only rise to the occasion when things are going well for them.

Having said that, however, I must also pay tribute to one of their swimmers, who showed sportsmen everywhere a wonderful example of the true Olympic spirit. Christine Caron was the first qualifier and a deserved favourite to win the Ladies' 100 metres back-stroke in Tokyo. 'Kiki', as she was known to everyone in swimming, was the idol of the French sporting public and seemed to enjoy her prima donna status, to which she brought all the supposed temperament of those operatic ladies. In the Olympic final she was beaten by a touch by the American girl, Kathy Ferguson, and we wondered how she would react to her narrow defeat. She behaved most graciously, however, and when, as the victory anthem was being played, the young American burst into tears, it was the disappointed silver medalist who reached up from the second step of the rostrum to take the winner's hand and squeeze it. A great gesture.

The same reporters who had rubbed me the wrong way in Blackpool twelve months earlier were now very full of Gottvalles's world record and were constantly eliciting opinions from me and volunteering ones of their own. Eventually I gave them the gist of my thoughts, as explained above, and finished by saying I thought Gottvalles *might* be second, but that he would probably be fourth or fifth.

The reaction from Gottvalles was better than I had hoped. On the day of the final he was quoted in the papers as saying that he did not mind who won, as long as McGregor was beaten. This added to my own confidence, for I could not imagine anyone being a formidable opponent who had such a negative attitude. In my opinion, he was beaten before he lined up.

The American sprinters, however, presented a much more daunting prospect. They were all good competitors, and although none of their three qualifiers had ever swum as fast as I had, I knew they would all be in close contention 'at the death'. There was little to choose between them on form, but Schollander was an outstanding stamina performer, being the world record-holder over 400 metres, and he was the only swimmer in the final whom I did not want near me with ten metres to go.

I spent a pleasantly relaxed race day, keeping mostly to myself and avoiding the other finalists. I was sure I could win and wanted to by a significant margin of perhaps three- or four-tenths of a second. But I was also sure that I would swim faster than I had ever done before, probably 53·3 or 53·4 seconds.

It was in this ultra-confident state of mind that I stepped on to the poolside of the magnificent Olympic swimming stadium. I took up my position behind lane 2, officially the position for the fifth fastest qualifier, although my 54·3 seconds was in fact the equal third fastest time with Gottvalles and

Austin, who had qualified earlier than myself. Ilman (53·9) and Schollander (54·0) were on lanes four and five respectively.

I looked down the fifty-metre stretch of glass-like water, and as usual the far wall looked a very long way off, but as I stood on the block I willed it closer.

The only clear impressions that remain of the minute that followed are a feeling that the race had gone well, although my turn could have been better. I remember feeling dreadfully exhausted over the final few metres and seeing Schollander at the wall with me, while the others were still finishing. Through the haze of fatigue which resulted from asking my body for everything that it had to offer, I was aware as I floated on my back in the water that my starting-block was bare, uncluttered by the official photographers who would inevitably have stormed the winner's lane.

I dropped my head and eyes backwards under the water as I felt myself enveloped in a black, sickening despair, which seemed to dwarf any other emotion I had ever experienced. I knew the silver medal must have been mine, but it meant nothing to me and at that precise moment I would willingly have swopped it for a double Scotch or a ticket home.

Perhaps the mere thought of my national drink helped me pull myself together for I quickly realized that this was what sport was all about, and that the Olympic Games were no place for adolescent petulance. I ducked under the ropes and was soon at Schollander's side in his lane. My congratulations were sincere, as I am sure was his reply, 'Yesterday or tomorrow, Bobby, it could've been you.' As later events proved, he was as much a prophet as he was a great sportsman.

He had won by one-tenth of a second, the smallest margin possible, in a new Olympic record time of 53·4 seconds, which was an astonishing half a second faster than he had ever swum before. My own time of 53·5 seconds was only slightly better than my previous best of 53·9 for 110 yards, which disappointed me, for I had hoped and expected to find something extra in my greatest test.

Schollander had defeated me in the manner in which I had feared he might, by exploiting my major weakness – a slight lack of stamina caused by never having competed over the middle distances.

I had gone up the first fast and easy, as I intended, and had taken the lead immediately after the turn. At that stage Schollander had been a good metre behind in third or fourth place.

I put on my greatest pressure during the third quarter and knew by the seventy-five-metre mark that I had dropped both Gottvalles and Ilman on my right and that only Schollander, invisible beyond these two, could possibly beat me. From that point to the end I concentrated on hanging on and I was conscious only of remaining ahead of my immediate rivals until the inevitable agony and near blackout of the final few metres.

Schollander had in fact been constantly behind me, although gaining, until exactly five metres out, at which point he overhauled me and held on more strongly than I to the wall.

He later went on to win the 400 metres freestyle and two relay gold medals, which made him justifiably the most successful Olympic swimmer of all time.

I must have looked very dejected and in need of consolation when the Olympic presentation ceremony was being held, for in the ten days following the final, I was inundated by some 500 fan letters from Japanese girls who had seen me on television. Most of them were invitations to visit their families, but many also suggested less formal surroundings. I also received so many calls at all hours of the day and night that the situation became intolerable and the main telephone exchange at the Olympic Village was instructed not to accept calls for me, unless they came from members of the British team or the British community in Tokyo. When the competitions were over, however, I did accept several invitations from the extremely friendly Japanese.

The widespread publicity which I had received had one very surprising and amusing sequel. During the short time I spent in London before returning home to Falkirk, I was approached at my hotel by a gentleman representing a businessman in the north of England. He explained that his client had seen me several times on television and had been so impressed by my looks and physique that he wanted to offer me the opportunity of becoming a professional wrestler! He apparently had the necessary influence with the promoters, who could guarantee me a considerable income. There was no question of his becoming my agent, he merely wanted to present me with an opportunity of capitalizing on my athletic fame, when I retired, as he thought I was soon to do.

I said I could not believe it was a serious offer, but my go-between insisted that it was and our meeting ended with me explaining that although I was genuinely touched by the proposition, I would consider meeting the likes of Jackie Pallo or Mick McManus only if all my bouts were held in deep water and without ropes!

The day after this I attended a reception at Buckingham Palace. I was introduced to the Royal Family and was surprised at the detailed knowledge of the swimming events shown by Her Majesty the Queen. She was very sympathetic about my narrow defeat and delighted me by remarking that I would have won if I had had longer fingernails.

My own townspeople also made me realize, in overwhelming fashion, that an international sportsman is never alone, no matter how far he may be from home. I will never forget the extent and warmth of my reception in Falkirk when thousands of my fellow-citizens cheered my progress to a civic celebration at the Town Hall. Such things are more valuable than medals, no matter what the metal.

5a. A study in concentration of the 1964 Olympic team coach Bert Kinnear and myself during a training session at Crystal Palace.

I am watching an incoming swimmer as I prepare for a relay take-over

5b. A good study of how it is possible to have unrestricted breath while swimming front-crawl, provided that the timing and head position are correct

5c. Relaxed and happy after winning the 110 yards freestyle in a new world record at the British Olympic Trials in 1964

6. Hans Klein (W. Germany), Donald Schollander (U.S.A.), and Bobby McGregor (Great Britain) just after the presentation for the Olympic 100 metres freestyle (1964) No bitterness from me, in spite of the narrowness of my defeat. But if only Schollander had been satisfied with his three other gold medals!

X. The Second Time Around

My failure to win the gold medal in Tokyo had a marked affect on me. I had no intention of continuing until the Mexico Olympics of 1968, so there seemed to be no possibility of establishing myself for posterity as one of the world's leading sprinters of my time. The Olympic results alone carry the 'official' stamp of an international sportsman's merit, regardless of what may happen during the years before and after the Games.

Perhaps it may seem rather vain to think in terms of 'posterity', and, of course, that sort of vanity was never the basic impetus of my swimming, but when one has worked hard for, and narrowly failed to achieve, the ultimate status in one's chosen activity, perhaps it is a forgivable vanity.

After Tokyo I decided that my swimming in the future would have less dedication than in the past. I was nearly twenty-one, and I wanted to be more free from the routine of training and the tensions of international competition. I took a whole year off and lived a more normal life, which included a six-week Continental camping holiday with three student friends. I had long wanted to travel rough, unfettered by etiquette and protocol, but by the end of our erratic wanderings around Europe I was totally re-converted to luxury travel with all its ancillary comforts.

In November 1965 I was mentally and physically refreshed and I recommenced training for the 1966 season, which included the Commonwealth Games in Jamaica and the Euro-

F

pean Games in Utrecht. It was four years since I last embarked on a season with these same major objectives, but I intended to make this second excursion a much more successful one than the first.

I found that I wanted to train as hard as ever, but with my developing maturity, I placed my swimming in an even truer perspective than before. I still wanted to be the best, I still wanted medals, I still wanted world records, but now I aspired to them with a more realistic understanding of where they came in the order of human values. I vowed I would never again expose myself to the inflated disappointment which had momentarily twisted my reasoning in Tokyo. Bobby McGregor, the boy, swam from 1960 to 1964, but I think the man took over in 1966.

Early in the year I competed for the first time in the German Indoor Championships at Bremen. It was my first competitive appearance for sixteen months, but I won the 100 metres in 52·9 seconds, which equalled the world record of Gottvalles. My swim could not be officially recognized, as the Bremen pool was only 25 metres long, but in spite of that it was an encouraging comeback.

I was hoping for a similar long-course performance in the Six Nations match a few weeks later, but my plans were upset by one of the most surprising and unpleasant experiences of my life.

I caught an apparently normal dose of influenza, which caused me to cancel my immediate competitions. I restarted training too early, however. This resulted in a bout of depression during which I had little enthusiasm for anything and I was also plagued by a recurring dream in which I committed suicide in a variety of excruciating ways! I explained the symptoms to my doctor and he relieved me by explaining that it was not an uncommon complaint, but that it might take some months to shake off the virus completely.

His diagnosis was accurate. I had a recurrence of the listlessness, depression and nightmares several times in the following nine months and I still ask myself whether what proved to be an outstandingly good season might have been even better.

For the Commonwealth Games in Jamaica in July, the Scottish Games Committee appointed me captain of the entire Scottish contingent, and I was determined to set the right example to my team-mates in every respect. Winning the 110 yards freestyle seemed as good a way as any, so I carefully re-examined the mistakes I had made in Perth four years earlier. I tried to avoid excessive sunbathing and socializing, but found it difficult to eliminate the latter, since as captain I was obliged to attend a large number of receptions. In spite of this, however, my race preparations went well and I felt fit and poised when the events began.

When the final of the sprint arrived, I already knew that it was not going to be an easy race. I had watched the sixteen-year-old Australian Mike Wenden set a world 220-yard record the previous day and I knew he was stronger, fitter and had more stamina than I, but I did not think these factors would outweight my advantage in sheer speed. I was wrong. Wenden led from start to finish and won in 54 seconds with myself a fifth of a second slower.

I was more annoyed with myself than disappointed. This was a very different situation from the Olympic final, for then Schollander had swum faster than I had ever done. But I had equalled Wenden's winning time on three occasions previously and beaten it once and my experience should have been enough to guarantee an optimum performance and tip the balance in my favour.

I had the greatest respect for Wenden, however, and did not in the least begrudge him his victory. He was no stylist and it was obvious that his performances could only be the fruits of far more exacting training than I had ever attempted, requiring great tenacity and willpower.

Angry though I was with myself over the result, I was much more upset by the attitude of some members of the British Press.

It was irritating enough to be headlined 'Mr Silver Medal' and 'Swimming's perpetual runner-up', but when one writer suggested that I should think of retiring and another that I might not want to go to the European Championships in Utrecht, I almost did feel like hanging up my trunks. My confidence was shaken for the only time in my career. I knew that in terms of consistent high-quality performances, I was the best sprinter in the world, but I began to think that perhaps there was something of a 'jinx' on me when it came to major events.

Luckily the Commonwealth Games are the easiest of all international sports festivals in which to lose one's sorrows in magnificent hospitality. I am reminded of what the great American golfer Walter Hager apparently said: 'I don't want to be a millionaire, I just want to live like one!' So it was with us in Jamaica. We were free of responsibilities after the competitions were over and yet we had a millionaire's playground at our disposal. A wealthy Scottish exile put a convertible car and motor launch entirely at my disposal and I spent glorious days sightseeing, water-skiing, and aqua-lung diving at a sunken city off Port Royal.

I had never dived before and during my second attempt I was foraging quite alone in rather murky water about thirty feet down when I felt something grip my shoulder. I swung round terror-stricken, expecting to be confronted by an octopus or some sea monster. Instead I found myself staring at about six inches range into the black face of the nine-year-old Jamaican boy who had accompanied myself and my host's daughter on our expedition. As we had only one aqualung in the boat, I had not expected to be accosted by another human six fathoms down, but he had dived down under his own steam to inform me that I should return to the surface. I did so with red face and thumping heart!

Another Scottish swimmer, Andy Harrower, and myself had struck up a great friendship with Mary Rand and Lilian Board, and we often attended parties as a foursome. Both these star athletes were fun to be with and, like ourselves, they wanted to take advantage of the social amenities now that the racing was over.

We arrived back at camp one night after a party and decided to have a moonlight swim in the pool. We collected our gear and had been enjoying the peaceful freshness for only a short time when the silence was broken by the sound of bawdy songs being sung in a robust and tipsy manner. Eventually four New Zealand weight-lifters appeared at the poolside. All four of us retreated to the dark shadows at the far side of the pool, but remained in the water.

' 's water nice?' inquired one of the weight-lifters. 'Rather cold,' said Mary Rand. 'Girls!' shouted one of the others, and at once proceeded to strip naked, before hurling himself into the water, barely a jock-strap ahead of his three similarly unclad companions.

Mary and Lilian departed the scene with a speed which would have done justice to any of their international appearances, while Andy and I maintained a respectable distance between ourselves and the intruders. Our diversionary measures allowed the girls to make good their escape, but it was not without risk to ourselves, for our new bathing companions were not in the least amused when they came close enough to discover our real sex!

That was not my only encounter with what are colloquially known in sporting circles as the 'heavies', although the second incident had more serious repercussions.

About 3 a.m. one morning I was awakened by the noise of fireworks exploding apparently right outside my window. On investigating I found that they were indeed going off near my ground-floor window, but were being dropped from a third-floor bedroom above.

Most of the Scottish block was now awake with the continuing din and I was approached by Dunky Wright, our team manager, and asked in my capacity as team captain to try to pacify three boxers who were the cause of the trouble. Dunky had already tried and failed, due perhaps he thought to the schism which sometimes exists between a team and its officials. He hoped that I, being 'one of the boys', might succeed.

The success of my attempt at mediation exceeded Dunky's only in so far as I was greeted with slightly less abuse, but I too was relieved to beat a fairly hasty retreat. The noise continued for some time before it finally ceased and the next morning two of the boxers were found to be unconscious. One of them was in a dustbin and the other in his room. As a result of complaints from other teams, two of the boxers were sent home, a stern sentence, but thoroughly deserved in this case, more for their selfishness than their condition. Although they themselves had finished competing, a team-mate in the next room was boxing the following day, as were several other sportsmen.

But there remains one cloud on the otherwise sunny perspective which Jamaica presented. Never before or since have I experienced such friction between black men and white men.

I first sensed that all was not well when I visited the palatial home of my host and his daughter. All the windows were barred and every room seemed to have a firearm of some kind prominently displayed. When I first sat in the convertible which I was loaned, I was shown a position under the dashboard, where a gas-gun was permanently stored. Such measures seemed frightening and unnecessary, but I soon found that they were in keeping with the social climate.

One afternoon I turned the car along a fairly busy side street not far from the main thoroughfare of Kingston, the capital. I had barely changed gear when I realized that we were being shouted at by people standing in the many doorways. I drew up, thinking perhaps it was a one-way street, and to my horror we were immediately surrounded by several thugs who began to beat myself and my two male companions about the head, while at the same time they lewdly insulted the three girls in the rear of the car.

I somehow managed to put the car in gear and roared off, just before two of our attackers could succeed in removing a watch from the wrist of my friend. As I discovered later, incidents like these were not uncommon, and even the native policemen seemed to take a delight in being extremely hard on the white Games participants.

On the day of the closing ceremony a policeman discovered Gordon Black (youngest brother of Ian) shinning up a flag pole with the obvious intention of taking the flag as a souvenir. We watched in amusement as he was ordered down, but our laughs turned to shouts of indignation as the law officer struck him several times with a heavy truncheon, although Black had said nothing, and had offered no resistance. Several members of the Scottish and English swimming teams including myself went to his assistance and I am still surprised at the restraint we showed in not giving the policeman some of his own medicine.

My enjoyment of the social life in Jamaica after the Games had to a great extent submerged my intense disappointment at not winning the sprint title. During the long journey home, however, my early misgivings about my performances in major events began to reassert themselves and I arrived back in Falkirk in anything but the best frame of mind for the European championships, which were then only a few days away.

I was able to spend only twenty hours with my parents between the two competitions, but it was long enough for my father and I to have a long talk and although still slightly depressed I was in a much more determined state of mine when I arrived in Utrecht, where I knew I had to prove myself.

It was obvious that the Russian sprinter Leonid Ilichev would provide the major challenge for the gold medal, for he had swum 53·5 seconds, the same time as I had done in Tokyo, when he had been narrowly defeated by Schollander in Moscow only five weeks earlier. He was similar to Wenden in that he was unusually strong rather than stylish, and at eighteen he also seemed very much younger than myself. Was I too old at twenty-two? The thought obsessed me and I sensed as I stepped on to my block for the final that this could be the last international race of my career.

Ilichev was on my right and Horst Gregor of East Germany on my left. The starting had not been particularly good during the championships and, probably due to lack of confidence in the starter, Ilichev began to overbalance. I stayed firm as the Russian managed to steady himself, but Gregor dived just before the pistol shot. I began to stand up, thinking it was bound to be a false start, but on realizing almost in the same instant that everyone else was following Gregor into the water, I too completed a late and very unsatisfactory dive. When I broke into my stroke I was a good yard behind Ilichev and it struck me at once, that if I lost this race it might appear that I had intentionally slow-started in order to have an excuse for being defeated.

Whether this bitterness had any effect on my performance or not, I was certainly driven up that first length by a desperation I had never experienced before. I was nearly alongside Ilichev at the turn and ten metres later I took a slight lead which I steadily increased until I hit the wall in 53·7 seconds, six-tenths of a second ahead of the Russian.

I was in no doubt that I had won the gold medal, for I watched all the other competitors finish, yet I experienced no great feeling of elation, merely a deep satisfaction that I had finally won the prize that could just have easily been mine in any of my three previous major international swims.

It was not that I in any way lacked respect for Pound, Schollander or Wenden, who had thwarted my gold medal attempts in the past, but every sprinter knows that when one is dealing in such minute measurements as tenths of a second, luck, in any of its many forms, can be the deciding factor on a particular day. Consistency of performance is the only sure way of always being in the scramble for first place and it was my consistency which was rewarded in Utrecht, in spite of a bad start and in spite of having faced Ilichev, who had performed fast enough to win the race only a short time before.

At about the same time that I was reaching for the gold medal in Utrecht my family at home in Falkirk were seeing an unexpected flash of the race on television. The BBC had been showing a half-hour of recorded highlights early each evening, but on the day of the 100 metres final they had apparently had a minute or two to spare between two programmes at the exact time when the race was about to begin. They had therefore immediately linked to Utrecht, hoping to cover the 100 metres live, as a bonus for all concerned. Unfortunately the start was delayed and normal programmes had to be rejoined when the race was barely half-way through its course.

Seeing me trailing the field after forty metres, my parents made frantic telephone calls to the BBC in Glasgow, then London and finally to a newspaper office, hoping to hear the final result, but no one seemed to know. It was not until I myself telephoned half an hour later, that their frustration was relieved.

Although my Tokyo time was on paper two-tenths of a second faster, my Utrecht swim was almost certainly the fastest 100 metres of my career, if one takes the time from my feet leaving the block till my final hand touch. Photographs of the dive and the distance I was behind once in the water made it quite clear that I lost at least half a second at the start and my 'real' time must therefore have been no worse than 53·2 or 53·3 seconds. The same photographs confirmed what everyone at the pool (except the starter!) also knew, namely that Gregor had definitely false-started and that everyone should have been recalled.

The French Press had its usual 'dig' at me in a cartoon which depicted a rather straight-faced McGregor on the rostrum receiving the gold medal. It was captioned 'Try a little smile, McGregor. Just imagine you're at the Olympic Games!' I loved that sort of publicity, because it showed I was still a thorn in their flesh. The time to worry would be when they felt they could justifiably ignore me.

But it was the Swedish reporters and photographers who gave the most comprehensive coverage of my exploits in Utrecht although the activities which they highlighted had little to do with swimming.

Utrecht saw the beginning of a two-year 'love affair' between myself and the Swedish girls' swimming team. I had always found them overpoweringly attractive, whenever Britain had one of our frequent matches with Sweden, but now perhaps, at twenty-two, I was succumbing to a young man's natural instincts after several years of comparative dedication to athletic ideals. Whatever the reason, however, my stay in Utrecht was all the more pleasurable as a result of the company of the Swedes, and my swimming performances were apparently not in the least affected by my frequent dating! Photographs of myself with a variety of Swedish beauties appeared in several Swedish newspapers and one had the following headline: '*Alla Sex Far Medalge*' – which had my mother frantically reaching for the Swedish phrase book!

The attitude of the Swedes, to me and to each other, was refreshingly mature. They seemed to accept happily that a young man should not escort the same girl all the time and my innocent 'girl-hopping' caused no ill-feeling among the girls, nor, even more surprisingly, among the Swedish officials or men swimmers.

British girl swimmers, on the other hand, do not enjoy quite as carefree a life when they are competing away from home. Our basic national character and education is very different from that of the Swedes, but in any case, even if some of our girls did want to 'play around', they would find it almost impossible under the British system of strict chaperoning.

Now it may seem that international sportsmen spend a disproportionate amount of time enjoying themselves, but it should be understood that most of the year is given over to strict training, and when the big event is over it is essential to let one's hair down and partake of the fruits which have been forbidden for a long time.

The brevity of these relationships which spring up at international sports meetings is one of the principal factors of their particular appeal. Competitors meet each other under artificial, rather glamorous circumstances, when everyone is putting on his best face, and before any kinks have time to develop the partners are usually flying off with nothing but the sweetest memories.

This type of affair, however, gave me an insight into the personalities of some outstanding sportswomen. Too often I uncovered an aggressiveness in their characters which, I am sure, would eventually make marriage a battle for supremacy between the husband and wife. It seems to me also that such girls would find it very difficult to adjust to the role of housewife when the glamour of international sport had been left behind.

It was only when I returned from Utrecht that I became aware of the extent to which my victory there had been publicized by the Press and the BBC. I was feted once again in my home town and received many invitations to judge beauty competitions and make similar personality appearances throughout the country. I was featured in articles in national magazines and newspapers and made several television appearances, but I continued my training and it was against this background of public support that I arrived at Blackpool for my final race of the year at the National Championships.

In August I had lost the world 110-yard record to the East German Frank Wiegand, who had clocked 53·7 seconds, and shortly afterwards in Canada the American Zac Zorn had reduced it by a further tenth of a second during a meeting in which Schollander had failed in an attempt to better the record. Having broken this record on four occasions in the previous few years, I was determined to regain it at Blackpool.

I could not have wished for a better setting or a more inspiring atmosphere than was provided by the Derby baths on the final evening of the 'Nationals'! I felt a surge of confidence as soon as I walked into the blaze of the arc lights and looked down the shimmering stretch of water which had been so lucky for me in the past. I concentrated on my father's final instructions. 'Go out faster than ever before, and hang on.' I did exactly that and came home in a new world record of 53·5 seconds.

The official announcement was greeted by a roar from the audience which surpassed any ovation I had ever received, and in those few minutes immediately after my effort the swimming public succeeded where I myself had failed, in driving from my mind all my rueful memories of Schollander and Wenden. I felt I had now established myself as the world's leading sprinter and the season closed with me brimful of confidence and eager to prove myself against anybody who felt like throwing down the gauntlet.

XI. Enjoyment and Indecision

As it turned out I did not have long to wait before my first challenge arrived in the form of an invitation to take part in two races a week apart at the annual Hall of Fame meeting at Fort Lauderdale, Florida. The Hall of Fame is unique in the sporting world. It is a million-pound complex consisting of a museum containing all kinds of memorabilia connected with the history of swimming, a lecture hall, dining-room and a fifty-metre outdoor pool. Each year a swimming festival is held there between 27 December and 3 January.

Linda Ludgrove from London and Jill Slattery from Sheffield, the Commonwealth back-stroke and breast-stroke gold medallists, were also invited, together with coach and swimming writer the late Bill Juba. On our arrival in Fort Lauderdale, which describes itself as the 'Venice of America' because of the profusion of sun and water, it was immediately apparent that the occasion was as much a social one as a competitive one. This suited me admirably, for I had broken a bone in my foot in September and the plaster had been removed only a few weeks earlier, so my fitness was not what it should have been. Moreover, I had probably reached my zenith as a swimmer with my world record three months earlier and my aim was now to enjoy myself till I retired at the end of the 1967 season. The Olympic Games would then be only a year away, but 1968 was also the year of my final examinations at university and I could see no way of tackling them successfully and at the same time training sufficiently to attain the physical condition which the Olympic Games demanded.

For these reasons I enjoyed the distractions that this winter resort offered and was unworried about my first race a few days after my arrival. Everybody, particularly my future opponents, seemed to stress that as these were out-of-season competitions, the outcome was of little importance.

During this trip I struck up a great friendship with Luis Nichlao, the Argentinian butterflier, whom I had met in Tokyo, and I soon discovered that he led a Jekyll and Hyde existence, as an international swimmer by day and international playboy by night. The day before my first race we were approached by two attractive American college girls who made it quite clear that they wanted our company that night. They told us that many of the swimmers would be attending a Boxing Day party and that we would be certain of a good time. Although I was competing the next day, I relented and a few hours later we were all having a swinging time at a gathering, which included many of the swimming set, but none of the competitors.

I was introduced to whisky sour, a drink new to me, and before finally getting to bed about 3 a.m., had consumed about ten measures, which had their inevitable effect on someone accustomed to only an occasional drink at Christmas or Hogmany.

I was still fully clothed when I awoke in my hotel room the next morning, and as I did not want anything to eat I went straight to the pool. A few hundred yards of easy swimming in the warm, clear water worked its usual miracle, for my physical co-ordination seemed fully restored and I soon succeeded in convincing myself that it was only an informal meeting after all. I ate a light lunch and relaxed till my race at 2 p.m.

Several of my sprint rivals knew of my outing on the previous night and they lost no time in pointing out that it was bound to affect my performance in the water. I laughed off their obvious attempts at gamesmanship and did an exaggerated act of being utterly carefree and unworried. Whether my attitude had a greater affect on them or me is a moot point, but it certainly seemed to do me no harm, for I won, easing up more than three yards ahead of the field, in the good time of 54·3 seconds.

I was naturally pleased that my first appearance in the United States had been a successful one, but I was also very surprised at my performance, because I had expected much less, especially after a hard night out.

The circumstances of my victory brought to my mind another story involving Walter Hagen. He was once asked why he was still up drinking and playing poker at 3 a.m., when his next day's opponent had been in bed for several hours. 'Sure, he's in bed,' he drawled, 'but he ain't sleepin'!'

As I walked back to the changing-room after the presentation Luis Nicolao grabbed my arm and indicated two of the men whom I had just defeated. They were being affectionately consoled by the same two girls whose acquaintance we had made the previous day! Having won the event I considered their 'Mata Hari' activities had already been suitably countered, but I resolved to humiliate their boyfriends even more in the second race a week later. I resisted my inclination to accompany Luis on his continuing round of the night clubs and prepared myself for the next encounter strictly according to the book.

As I stood behind my block a few days later, fresh, composed, well-rested and confident, I had visions of a best-ever performance from myself of something around 53 seconds plus. I had expected nothing like that before leaving home, but now my logic seemed reasonable: I had eased up about half a second in the first race, I had probably lost half a second due to not preparing myself properly the night before, and on top of that I was now much more determined.

But it was not to be, for I swam my slowest international race for four years and although I still managed to win in 55 seconds, it was only after a desperate finish in which Steve Rerych and Zac Zorn clocked 55 seconds and 55·2 seconds respectively.

I was baffled by the wide variation in effort and time between my two swims, but concluded that perhaps we are inclined to exaggerate the affect of 'non-training' behaviour on the fit athlete. His fitness probably makes him less susceptible than the non-athlete to minor physical indiscretions, provided his psychological condition remains healthy. I thought again of my Cockney team-mate at Leipzig in 1962 and for the first time realized that possibly his behaviour was less reprehensible than I had always believed!

But in spite of my very close call in the second event, I had made a great impression on the Americans. I was asked to swim a lap of honour and was announced as 'the world's fastest human in the water'. This gave me a wonderful boost, for the Americans were obviously giving me credit for my competitiveness and high-level consistency in winning races. They knew that the world metric record of 52·9 seconds was relatively speaking slightly faster than my own linear record, yet they still regarded me as the fastest.

Within a week their opinion had been made official, for I was named as the World No. 1 for 100 metres freestyle by the American magazine *Swimming World*. This was the result of a poll of international swimming writers, coaches and officials, and in that it was a decision of my peers in swimming, people whose judgement was universally respected, it was my greatest honour within the sport.

That was one of my great moments, but the greatest had come a few days earlier, when I had received a telegram from home informing me that I was to be awarded the M.B.E. in the New Year's Honours List. I felt dazed as I read it. It seemed almost unfair that anyone should be awarded such an honour for doing something which he immensely enjoyed anyway, and which had already brought ample rewards in terms of world travel and interesting experiences.

I was treated to a celebration dinner party by film stars Esther Williams, Buster Crabbe and Johnny Weismuller, all three former world-famous swimmers, who always visited the Hall of Fame meeting. The evening was highlighted by one particular amusing incident involving Johnny Weismuller, who

7a. My parents with some of the trophies of success . . .

7b. . . . but who needs medals when there are rewards like this – the scene outside my home on my return from Tokyo (1964)

8. The picture which proves that the European 100 metres final began with a false start (1962). After a legitimate start no swimmer could have been in the water so far ahead of all the others as Gregor (E. Germany) is in the photograph. I was even further behind only because, being next to him I knew he was obviously false-starting and I waited, thinking he must be recalled

had been telling us that he often recognized his own yell and some action shots of himself in recent Tarzan films, although he had ceased to play the role some years before. When we left the nightclub at about 2 a.m., I asked him to demonstrate his yell in the early-morning stillness of Miami Beach. Complete extrovert and great sport that he is, he clambered up the portico of a hotel and against a background of swaying palms, he opened his throat and let loose. Within seconds a uniformed porter trotted into view out of the trees and inquired angrily, 'Say, bud, who d'ya think you are, Tarzan?' He was at a loss to understand our helpless laughter until Johnny presented all 6 ft 4 in and 15 stone of himself at close quarters with words, 'Yes, me Tarzan.' Although he was then sixty-two years old, he still bore a striking resemblance to his younger image of the cinema screen and the porter recognized him instantly. Reaching open-mouthed into his tunic pocket he produced a snapshot of a family group, and proffering the blankside, asked for the autographs of Johnny and of Buster Crabbe, whom he had also recognized as the star of many 'Flash Gordon' films.

Unfortunately, Esther Williams had left earlier, so at the insistence of my two famous companions the small space that remained on the photograph was filled by my autograph, although it was obvious that the porter could barely understand why I should be featured in such esteemed company.

In spite of the generally pleasant time that I had in Florida, however, there was one despondent moment. On New Year's Eve, or Hogmany as we term it in Scotland, I could find no one who was remotely interested in joining me in a Scottish-type celebration. At midnight, therefore, I sat alone in my hotel bedroom feeling desperately homesick for the first time in my life. Never has it been more obvious to me that I am first and foremost a Scot, rooted in our customs and traditions and damned proud of it! I must have seemed a candidate for the lunatic asylum as with tears running down my cheeks I sang Scots songs, threw a couple of streamers round the room and had

G

a couple of swigs from a bottle of whisky – only another Scot would understand my strange behaviour.

Determined though I was to enjoy myself during my last season in competitive swimming, I nevertheless wanted to quit at the top. I trained as hard as ever after my return from Florida. All my energies were directed towards a peak lasting from the end of August until the end of September, during which period I would have six major competitions. The final one was to be a Great Britain v. U.S.A. match, when I hoped to have an opportunity to turn the tables on my Olympic conqueror, Don Schollander.

My season opened at the beginning of June at Bergen in Norway, where I produced the best short-course sprinting of my career. I won an individual 100 metres in 53·3 seconds then in two team races I returned 52·6 seconds and 51·7 seconds. This latter time, even allowing for the flying start, was relatively speaking as good as anything I had done over a long course and I was staggered that I had managed it so early in the season. I was also slightly perturbed, however, for I wanted to save my best swims for the most important races three months later.

I mentioned these misgivings to my father, but he pointed out that I had long since reached the stage where my body soon tuned itself up to the optimum efficiency of the previous season. I should be delighted to swim so well without having specially peaked, for when I did peak an improvement should still materialize.

Immediately after this, I received an invitation to compete a few weeks later in a 100-metre event at the international invitation meeting in Santa Clara, California, the headquarters of the world's most successful swimming club.

I was extremely keen to take part in this race, for the field included Schollander and several other top Americans, but as often happens when one faces an important challenge, I had doubts about whether I could prepare adequately in the time available; but as Schollander's coach, George Haines, suggested in his letter of invitation that Don probably would not be in the squad due to come to Britain in late September, I knew I had to accept this invitation or risk losing for ever my chance of squaring matters with the Olympic champion.

I arrived in California a few weeks later and found that this return match between Schollander and myself had aroused tremendous interest throughout the whole of the United States. This was most unusual for a swimming event, because sports such as athletics and swimming have no mass public following in America, in spite of the unsurpassed international success of American competitors. Only baseball and American football have any wide appeal and they monopolize the Press and television to an even greater extent than soccer and cricket do in this country.

On the strength of his four gold medals at Tokyo, however, Schollander had been voted American Sportsman of the Year in 1964, and the narrowness of his 100 metres victory was apparently still fresh in the public memory. There were numerous television interviews featuring the two of us in the days before the meeting and Don himself confirmed that he had never known a swimming race receive such publicity.

In terms of tension it was the Olympic final all over again. Schollander had the advantage of swimming in his home pool in familiar circumstances, but I felt that the great publicity given the meeting was to my advantage, because it increased the pressure on him. He knew that the public expected him to win, but he also knew that the race was every bit as open as it had been in Tokyo. The pre-race situation was in fact the reverse of the Olympic final when I had been the favourite.

I have never willed myself to relax as I did before that race. Schollander was much more nervous than he had been in Tokyo and the other experienced and high-quality American sprinters were also obviously under pressure. For them it was an opportunity to grab greater glory than ever before.

The pool was surrounded by 6,000 spectators, but more than twice that number saw the race, for a hill which overlooks the pool provided a perfect natural grandstand for several thousand more.

Schollander and I were in adjacent lanes and straight from the gun we swam as if locked together until ten metres from the end, when on this occasion it was I who managed to find enough to win by a fifth of a second in 53·8 seconds. Both of us had swum about half a second slower than our best, which was not surprising for this was a real pressure race, man to man, with a great deal at stake. In that situation one can dispense with watches, for they mean little in the context of the race.

It was my day, because Don tried to win so convincingly that he did not swim his normal race. He slightly over-extended himself in staying alongside me from the start in spite of my known superiority in pure speed. Had he swum the same race as in Tokyo he might have repeated his victory. He realized this after the race, but he was extremely generous in defeat, like he had been in victory.

How much did my victory mean to me? Exuberance and elation were totally absent. I felt as if I were lying alone in the heather watching a beautiful sky after a twenty-five-mile hike. It was an ecstasy of peace and satisfaction.

Only after I returned to Britain did the full impact of my performance sink in, for only then did I consciously realize that, in Schollander and Zac Zorn, I had defeated two of the strongest challengers for the Olympic sprint in Mexico the following year; and for the first time I began gently to consider the possibility of competing for another year. I reached no decision at that time but success in the Californian sun certainly rekindled in me the Olympic flame which I had believed permanently extinguished.

In the four weeks following my trip to the United States I retained my Scottish 110-yard title in 54·4 seconds, won the 110 in an international match in 54 seconds dead, then retained my A.S.A. title also in 54 seconds dead. These world-class swims served as an excellent springboard for a return visit to Tokyo where I hoped further to eradicate my unhappy memories of the Olympic Games by winning the 100-metre gold medal at the World Student Games. I was sure my condition was as good as ever before, and I was as confident of winning as I had been three years before in the same pool.

After the heats and semi-finals, however, I realized that my passage might not be as smooth as I had imagined. Two Americans, Don Havens and Zac Zorn, both of whom I had defeated at Santa Clara, led the qualifiers with the same time of 53·2 seconds, so it seemed likely that at least one of them would produce a similar swim in the final. My own qualifying time was 53·9 seconds and although I had something in hand, I knew I would probably have to produce a personal best performance in order to win.

We were all 'pure' sprinters and for that reason it was very much a question of the gold going to the one who could 'hang on' till the wall. Zorn 'blew up' first, but Havens managed to maintain his impetus as I folded when in the lead a few metres from home. The American's winning time was 53·2 seconds and I was a fifth of a second slower.

Again I tasted the most bitter fruit of international sport. I once read that it was a triumph to reach the final of a major sports event and a consolation to win the bronze medal, but that the most agonizing and frustrating prize was the silver. That writer displayed a rare insight which few sportsmen can be better qualified to corroborate than myself. My disappointment was acute, but while I was still licking my wounds, it was the Americans again who rubbed salt in them by winning the three team races and thereby relegating my team-mates and myself to two more silver medals and one bronze! To be fair, of course, these last three performances were in effect a triumph for British swimming and represented our best international team performance for many years.

I was again assailed by the old doubts. Was I just unlucky in big events, or was I not as good a competitor as I imagined? I had never seriously considered the second possibility, but I did now and was disturbed by it.

From my own experience, however, I knew that poor competitors, and I had met many, were not usually narrowly defeated into second place. They were much more likely to 'chicken out' completely and finish down the field. By examining and dissecting my own competitive record I managed to rehabilitate myself psychologically and concluded that I would just have to soldier on and continue to 'play the averages'. I drew greatest comfort from the knowledge that I had broken 54·5 seconds for 100 metres more times than any other three or four sprinters in the world put together. Consistency was still my most powerful ally and I believed it was in the long run the most valuable one.

But I did not allow my disappointment to diminish the many attractions of Tokyo for which I had had neither the time nor the inclination during my first visit three years earlier. The atmosphere of a Student Games is perhaps the least formal of all such meetings. Once the competitions are over, the team members are virtually 'on their own' till the time of the flight home, and as nearly all the participants are more than eighteen years old, supervision is inclined to be cursory to say the least.

We managed to survive an inspection tour of the more lurid side of Tokyo's night life, and, three years later than intended, I enjoyed the supreme pleasures of a genuine Japanese bath. There is something wonderfully relaxing, and indeed morally cleansing, to be stripped naked by an attractive young girl for the unimpeachable motive of being washed. And there can be few more pleasurable sensations than the patter of tiny feet, when they are expertly tripping up and down your own spine!

Another happy memory of the Far East was our visit to a Japanese inn, where we were entertained in a garden restaurant to the most magnificent meal I have ever eaten. We sat cross-legged round a large table with a hot-plate in the centre on which two geisha-type ladies cooked mountains of succulent meats, fish, vegetables, soups, fruits and many other spiced delicacies which I could not identify. And all of this in a most beautifully quiet, fragrant setting, which gave one the impression of being in a kind of Shangri-La, isolated from the modern world with its noise and neuroses.

Finally there was the riotous final-night party at the Olympic Village, which culminated in the early hours with my watching three naked males and one naked female playing 'tag' on bicycles round the open-air swimming-pool. Eventually the female, an inveterate prankster and superb swimmer, terminated the proceedings by riding her bicycle off the three-metre board into the water. Understandably her 'follow-my-leader' antics found no takers among the men.

Immediately on my return from Tokyo I won the 100 metres sprint in the Six Nations match in Dortmund, clocking 53·9 seconds to the 54·6 seconds of the new French star Marc Rousseau. But the most significant performance of the match was the fine victory of our men's medley team. We had at last found a capable breast-stroker in Roger Roberts and with that long-standing weak link eliminated it was clear that our team of Roddy Jones, Roberts, Lenny Norris and myself could go close to winning a medal in Mexico the following year. It was this more than anything else that made me seriously consider continuing until the next Olympic Games. We had a fine spirit and great confidence in Bert Kinnear's ability to prepare us as a fighting unit for Mexico.

I had already realized that my chances of winning an individual gold would be very much less than in Tokyo, judging by the number of sprinters who were then capable of swimming under 54 seconds for the 100 metres, but it was an attractive thought not to be favourite. Indeed, if my principal motivation for competing lay in anchoring the team race, then I might be under much less pressure in the individual event.

My team-mates were constantly cajoling me to stick with them for another year and eventually, more by way of a joke than anything else, I agreed to commit myself to Mexico if we broke 4 minutes 4 seconds for the medley team race in the match against the Soviet Union two weeks after the Six Nations meeting. As this meant improving on our brand new British record by a further two seconds, I thought I was giving nothing away.

We travelled first of all to Moscow, then 1,200 miles south-wards to Tbilisi, the capital of the State of Georgia. Conditions there were excellent for fast outdoor swimming and both teams rose to the occasion in the warm sunshine before capacity crowds.

The medley team race was my first swim of the two-day meeting and for several reasons it proved to be the most interesting and exciting team event of my career. Roddy Jones swam very well, but nevertheless was trailing the European champion Gromak by about a yard at the end of the back-stroke leg. We expected Roger Roberts to be thrashed on breast-stroke in spite of his newly-acquired excellent form, for the Russians had always been outstanding on this stroke, but Roberts amazed us by actually handing over a slight lead after the finest swim of his career. Unfortunately, Lenny Norris had an off-day on butterfly – exaggerated by the fact that he was meeting the European record-holder Gordeev, and I found myself four yards behind Gusev on the final leg. The Russian had a tremendously powerful leg-kick and as we had accidentally converged on each other with our starting dives, I found myself swimming in his turbulent wake. This was usually considered to be a disadvantage for the chasing swimmer, but on this occasion it seemed as if I was 'slip-streaming' the leader, for I felt myself being drawn up to him. At the turn I was only two yards down and the gap was still closing when the Russian hit the wall with myself six-tenths of a second behind.

Victory had eluded us, but we were all delighted by our new British record of 4 minutes 3·9 seconds which was also, of course, a tenth of a second inside the agreed time of the light-hearted bargain I had struck with the other boys. In fact, this final decision to train for Mexico could not have been given a better send-off in that my own official split in the team race had been 52·6 seconds, exactly equalling the three-week-old world record of the new American star Ken Walsh. I had had a flying start, of course, but it seemed that my time might actually have been even faster, for several unofficial watches, which were timing only my leg, recorded times ranging from 51·7 seconds to 52·3 seconds. After such encouragement, I could hardly wait for the individual 100 metres, so convinced was I that the world record, or at least my first sub-53-second swim, lay within my grasp.

The race, when it came, served only to expose the folly of trying to beat the clock instead of concentrating on beating the man. I set off rather like Schollander in our Santa Clara confrontation, as if I were swimming a 50-metre dash, and although I reached the turn faster than ever before, it had cost me dear. By the eighty-metre mark I felt as if a little man had climbed on my back, and from there till the finish I was more concerned with staying afloat than winning races!

The two Russians took full advantage of my agony in the latter stages and came very close to edging me into third place for the first time in any race since the international match in Budapest in 1962. Ilichev won in 53·7 seconds, Kulikov was third in 53·9 and I was sandwiched between them on 53·8 seconds.

Recovery from a well-paced sprint, no matter how much the swimmer has given, is usually fairly rapid, but the effects of a bad race linger on. I had a pain in my chest for a few hours afterwards and was almost too tired to be disappointed at what was my first defeat for Britain in an international match for more than five years.

The 1967 season was indeed full of the ups and downs which make sport such a valuable rehearsal for the more serious fluctuations which face us in life itself, but fortunately for me the 'ups' had outnumbered the 'downs' and the season finished on a highspot soon after our return from the Soviet Union, when I won the 110 yards for Britain against the United States at Crystal Palace. My time was 53·9 seconds and I had a considerable 1·1 seconds in hand over Steve Rerych.

It had also been a very busy year for me and through its mass of activity shone one or two flashes of brilliance which tantalizingly suggested that my Japanese Silver might possibly be superseded by Mexican Gold.

XII. Operation Mexico

Even before the 1967 season was at an end those swimmers who were considered likely to represent Britain in Mexico were involved in the National Olympic Training Plan. When it was first conceived more than a year before the Olympics, the plan represented a laudable and positive attempt to guarantee that Britain was well represented in Mexico. The scheme incorporated the formation of an Olympic Training Squad consisting of those swimmers who equalled or bettered certain standard times set by the G.B. Committee and the selected swimmers were to have many training sessions together at various venues, including some at altitude, to all of which individual coaches were to be invited. The idea had the enthusiastic support of almost everybody who was likely to be involved with it. The morale of our best swimmers was very good, for everybody could see that a genuine attempt was being made to give our competitors the kind of preparation they had never had before.

I was wholeheartedly behind the programme in the early stages, but it soon became apparent that there were many problems, the most important of which was the lack of a universally acceptable supremo to govern the training side of the scheme.

We had an excellent organizer in Norman Sarsfield, the Olympic Team Manager, but the vacuum left by the earlier resignation of the A.S.A.'s chief coach, Bert Kinnear, never came near to being filled and this left the most important part of the whole operation, the actual squad training, crying out for the inspired direction without which it could not function properly.

Hamilton Bland, a young and in the academic sense, very able coach, was appointed to Kinnear's position, and as such he automatically became the chief coach of the Olympic squad. He was about the same age as many of the swimmers under his control, but that in itself would not have been a major drawback if he had possessed the inspiring personality of a successful coach and the ability to command respect because of outstanding achievements either as a competitor or as a coach. Bland, with his limited experience, could not fairly have been expected to show these qualities. In short he was a likeable individual placed in an impossible position by the incompetence of the A.S.A.

As the Olympic captain designate and an experienced team member, I decided to give Bland my complete support and also to encourage the whole team to support him. That we failed in spite of the goodwill of many of the swimmers was entirely due to the total absence of it in some of the other coaches and swimmers who were involved in squad training.

Coaches, like any other group of people in any walk of life, all want to make professional progress, to reach the top of their particular tree and to have their own wide sphere of influence. It had taken Kinnear many years to reach a position where he was accepted by the British coaches. They may not always have agreed with him, but his authority, built up over the years, was such that any coach and swimmer would listen to him and work under him without experiencing a strong feeling that there were others who could do the job better. With the appointment of Bland this respect was understandably weakened and 'team' training in the real sense seemed to exist only in Norman Sarsfield's imagination.

I blame the A.S.A. for this blunder because it *was* foreseeable and, what is more important, avoidable. It should have been clear to the A.S.A. that there was no one of Kinnear's status and acceptability in Britain, and therefore they should have brought in a foreign coach, whose *proven* ability and experience would have ensured the widespread support of both swimmers and coaches in this country. There are several Australian and American coaches whose names spring to mind, and who for the kind of money that the A.S.A. could have afforded, would have come to Britain if not for the whole of 1968, certainly for the critical months of June, July, August and September, plus the few weeks in Mexico. There have been many examples of the success of this policy in other countries. The most outstanding were probably the achievements of the Dutch team under Australian Forbes Carlisle at the 1962 European Games, and the similarly excellent performances of the Mexicans under American Ron Johnson in 1968.

There are many of our own coaches who have what it takes to reach the same standards as the American and Australians, but there was no one at home whom everybody concerned with the British Olympic Squad would have respected enough to forget personal aspirations and jealousies. On the other hand, a troubleshooter of proven ability from abroad would have been above any existing personality problems, he would certainly have brought fresh and worthwhile ideas, and, perhaps most important of all, only an outsider would have had any possibility of unifying the factions which are constantly working against each other within British swimming.

What did happen was that Norman Sarsfield, who was the best team manager and organizer I ever met throughout my career, unfortunately took upon himself, albeit unofficially, the mantle of chief coach. This was an impossible task for one man, but in any case Sarsfield's reputation as a coach was not sufficiently outstanding to arouse in the squad that feeling of absolute confidence which is the essential ingredient of any successful coach/team relationship. Almost before it was launched, therefore, what had been in essence an excellent plan began to disintegrate.

In spite of these deficiencies, however, the scheme did generate a genuinely happy team spirit in the social sense, and if it had not been for the fact that we were supposed to be training for the Olympic Games, one would have had difficulty in finding any faults at all. A holiday trip to the Spanish mountains at Christmas was a much appreciated venture, probably unique in British amateur sport, and a similar visit to a luxury hotel in the Swiss Alps in the spring was also a great morale booster. These two episodes were inspired innovations into the rather unimaginative training pattern of previous British swimming teams. Yet in 1968 they had a negative result, in so far as their spectacular social success tended to divert attention from the training inadequacies which were developing.

Our visit to Spain was without doubt the most enjoyable 'training' I ever did, and by the end of our stay we would have soundly defeated any other swimming team in the world, provided that races had been measured in rum and cokes instead of minutes and seconds!

Our excellent hotel was a favourite resort for wealthy Spaniards and we lost no time in joining them in the well-known 'Apres-Ski' diversions of winter sports, which few of us could otherwise have afforded in such grand surroundings.

We could do no swimming, for although there was a swimming-pool it turned out to be an outdoor one, and, being situated several thousand feet up in the Sierra Nevada Mountains, it was frozen over. Our training, therefore, consisted only of long walks up the mountains and physical exercises at the hotel. By the end of our holidays, however, all of us had improved our fitness, according to the Harvard University step-up tests, so the sojourn at altitude did produce positive training results in spite of the nightly carousing which all the older swimmers found an outstanding feature of the holiday.

There were two occasions, however, when it momentarily appeared that the Olympic team had lost a swimmer – permanently!

We set off one day on a walking climb up a glacier which we had discovered, but not explored, on an earlier outing.

The higher we went the mistier it became, until eventually

visibility was down to a few yards, and although we had still not reached the summit, we reluctantly decided to return to base before we were hopelessly lost.

The downward journey proved much more perilous than we had imagined, for it was very slippery underfoot and we found it difficult not to travel too fast for safety. There were several minor falls or stumbles, but we thought we had avoided serious mishaps until Roger Roberts lost his balance and careered full-length down into the mists. We heard his big frame slithering away in the near distance and then silence.

He had vanished sideways off the glacier into territory which we had not previously covered and we all feared that he might have gone over a precipice. We shouted and were immensely relieved when he called out, apparently from about twenty yards distance. Roddy Jones and myself gingerly followed the course of his disappearance and eventually came to a ridge with only space beyond it. Gripping Jones's anorak as a makeshift rope I leaned forward and peered down. Roberts looked up from a mass of deep soft snow about four feet below me. 'Jump down, its great,' he beamed, 'like landing on a feather bed!'

The next half hour was a riot of fun, as the whole team re-traced his route in a series of individual races, both sitting, standing, and even some team races with the members locked together in the manner of a four-man bob sled! It was hard work climbing back after each slide, but our exertions must have improved enormously our resistance to the effects of altitude.

The other moment of tragic comedy had myself as the central character. The hotel had arranged a New Year's Eve party which proved to be such a swinging affair that I almost forgot it was not a Scottish Hogmanay. During the festivities hundreds of streamers were thrown and soon the floor was a foot deep in paper. A playful fight developed in which the guests were gathering up large armfuls and throwing them at each other. I slipped headlong at one stage and was lying on the floor when John Thurley, my room-mate, who like most of us was in a very tipsy condition, dropped a heap of streamers on me. Unfortunately, it contained an empty wine bottle, which caused a painful cut on my head. It was not a serious injury but together with the substantial amount of wine I had consumed it had the effect of making me feel distinctly groggy and I reluctantly decided to go to bed. I picked up my Olympic blazer which I had hung over a chair and was annoyed to find that someone had spilled food over it, so once back in my room, I filled the bath with water and spread my blazer and trousers in it to soak overnight.

A few minutes later I was startled from my half sleep by Thorley's voice shouting 'McGregor's drowned himself! He's drowned himself!' I arose as swiftly as throbbing head would allow and was confronted by my glassy-eyed team-mate who was leaning against the wall of the short entrance lobby of our apartment, staring fixedly into the unlit bathroom. His shouts had attracted the two girls in the room opposite ours, and being the only clear-headed individuals present they imediately took in the situation with much enjoyment, whereas John and I merely muttered at each other, myself annoyed at being roused and he apparently resentful I was still alive!

It was an understandably happy team which returned to Britain in early January and, still buoyant with the memory of our fun in the mountains, I am certain we all trained hard as we looked forward to our next trip in April to the French high-altitude camp in the Pyrenees.

It had been stressed in advance that the Spanish outing would be mainly a holiday and as no genuine altitude training had been done there, it seemed only logical that the few precious days at Font Romeu should have been used exclusively for some really demanding bulk training, but this was not what happened, for on the sixth and seventh days of the ten-day period an international match had been arranged with the Dutch national team. Their swimmers had been training for five days before our arrival, and were in peak condition having just completed a five-week tour during which they had competed several times.

9a. This is the kind of concentration and determination I always tried to show as I left the block

9b. Myself in full flight. Note the high head position and the relaxed, high-elbow arm recovery

9c. The happy ending to the near disaster of plate 8. My first gold medal victory, with Leonid Ilichev (Soviet Union) the silver medallist, on the left and Udo Poser (East Germany) the bronze medallist, on the right

10a. The scene at Santa Clara, California as the crowd builds up for the opening of the Annual International Invitation Meeting

10b. (right) Revenge at last! Both Don Schollander and myself look very calm, cool and collected on the rostrum after our return match in Santa Clara, but I was feeling much happier than this photograph suggests

10c. Santa Clara again – the presentation. On the extreme right is Steve Clark, who failed to win an individual place in the American Olympic team, yet who won three team-race gold medals

Not surprisingly we were defeated and as we had regularly and heavily defeated the Dutch in the past, the effect on team morale was anything but good. Apart, however, from the negative psychological effect of a defeat in our first competitive encounter as an Olympic training unit, the match was even more harmful in that it unbalanced what should have been an immensely valuable ten days of severe training. As it was, the first two days of the visit were taken up with acclimatization, then most of our team did a short 'taper' for the two or three days before the event in an effort to do a good performance. This meant that with the two days of competitions, about seven of the ten days at altitude were not used as advantageously as they might have been.

We did hear afterwards that it was necessary to have a match at altitude in order not to exceed the International Olympic Committee's regulation regarding the length of time allowed for altitude training. If this were the case it should have been made clear to the team in advance that it was more of a 'convenience' than a match, and treated as such, by not selecting anyone for their Olympic event.

In his report on the visit Norman Sarsfield said: 'Everyone was swimming better at the end of the trip, when *ideally the match should have been held*'; and also in reference to the intention to return to Font Romeu in June, he added, '*unencumbered by match problems*, a real massive programme of work will be attempted'. Should these problems not have been evident when the decision to hold the match was taken some months before? It was bad enough to place our team in a disadvantageous competitive position in which they had nothing to gain and everything to lose, but it was even more unfortunate to allow an unimportant contest to reduce the potentially enormous benefit of our first real training at altitude.

H

XIII. Olympic Selection

Soon after the match at Font Romeu we moved into the period during which it was possible for any swimmer to ensure Olympic selection by achieving any of the revised standard times which the G.B. committee had applied to each event. The four months beginning 1 April included five major competitions, in which most of the Olympic Training Squad were in action, and also three international invitation events for a few selected swimmers. This competitive build-up culminated in the A.S.A. championships at the beginning of August, when the Olympic team was to be announced. The basis for selection was simple, in that anyone who had equalled the fifth time in the final of any event in the Tokyo Olympics would be automatically selected for Mexico. If more than the permitted Olympic maximum of three swimmers qualified, then the results of the A.S.A. championship would be the deciding factor for that particular event.

These principles had been laid down many months before and there had been general agreement that they presented a fair and practicable selection policy. The intention had been to reduce the tremendous strain imposed on swimmers when a single trial decides who will be selected, and also to eliminate the one important disadvantage of the latter method, in that a star performer might do his only poor swim of the season at the trial and therefore fail to make the team.

Unfortunately, however, this bold experiment was a failure for all except the very small group who managed to achieve the target times fairly early in the season. Certainly the strain was removed from their shoulders, but the very much larger group of swimmers, who were just below the standard, found themselves under great tension for the whole period from April (the earliest qualifying date) until the A.S.A. championships. Several of our best swimmers were nervous wrecks by the time August arrived, as a result of trying to maintain peak form so that they could make persistent attacks on the set times throughout the exhaustingly long international season.

I have no wish to criticize anyone for this, for the difficulties I have mentioned, although obvious once the international season began, were less apparent when the overall plan was being formulated. But the whole business of team selection is so important that I wish to deal with it in detail and to make certain constructive suggestions, which I hope will reach those eight powerful gentlemen of the Great Britain Selection Committee.

To begin with, for the Olympic Games and similar events, one set of trials should be the principal basis for selection. I would never prescribe times which *automatically* gain selection, and although I believe there is a place for 'minimum requirement' times, I would calculate them and apply them quite differently from the method used by the British selectors for Mexico.

Both of these statements will find vigorous opponents, but I can answer the well-known objections.

In the first place, it is unfair to have selection times based arbitrarily on the performance of the swimmers who finished fifth in the finals of the previous Olympics. Assuming that the selectors are trying to be fair to all swimmers concerned on all strokes, the times selected as standards in this way presuppose two false premises: (1) that the performance of the fifth swimmer in one event is of identical, or at least similar quality to that of any swimmer, male or female, who was fifth in any other final, and (2) that all the events have improved at the same rate since the previous Olympics. The second point is much the more important of the two. The crux of the problem lies in the fact that it is impossible to equate in absolute terms a performance in one event with another performance in another event, and yet this is the bed-rock of a selectorial policy based on times. Inevitably, anomalies will arise, and that is something which the towering importance of once-in-a-lifetime Olympics selection must try to avoid.

There were several inconsistencies in Britain's qualifying times for Mexico, but perhaps the most obvious was the divergence in quality between the rather poor (by current international standards) ladies' 200 metres freestyle time of 2 minutes 20 seconds and the fairly good men's 200 metres back-stroke time of 2 minutes 15·7 seconds. Four girls managed the former time and all went to Mexico (although only three swam), yet not a single male back-stroker qualified for the trip, although David Butler won the British title in 2 minutes 16·3 seconds. At the Games themselves a girl returning 2 minutes 20 seconds would have failed by the large margin of 4 seconds to reach the final, while a back-stroker doing 2 minutes 15·7 seconds would have been fourth fastest qualifier for that final!

It is said, of course, that times give an incentive to swimmers to aim high, and this certainly sounds a convincing argument, but again it is based on the false, and indeed slightly derogatory belief that, but for the existence of set times, our competitors would not train hard enough for Olympic selection. My experience is that when really important selections are being considered all swimmers are giving of their maximum anyway, and a particular target time cannot make anyone give more than one hundred per cent.

If there were no standards, a star swimmer would not be so stupid as to ease off his training, because he felt confident of winning and therefore gaining selection regardless of his performance. He does not know how fast the other fellows are going in their training camps, and he must therefore train to his maximum ability for the big event.

But a more dangerous result of having selection times lies in the psychological leeway which they allow the swimmer. It is inevitable that, having achieved a certain prescribed time, the competitor should feel that whatever happens thereafter he has already done what was expected of him and deserved selection. I am not suggesting that an athlete would intentionally ease up and consider that his work was done, but at the back of his mind will be the realization that merely to repeat a particular performance at the Games will guarantee an official stamp of approval. I believe that an athlete's psychology should be 'open-ended' in relation to what he should achieve. If it is, he might well surprise himself.

Having rejected such times, how would I fairly select my Olympic team? I would rely almost entirely on one set of trials held at one venue over a period of a few days. The 'almost' is important because we do not have the quality of depth in this country to select automatically the first three in each event, regardless of other considerations.

This is of course the simplest of all methods of selection, but it is really only practicable in a country such as the United States where the abundance of athletic talent inevitably produces a superb team even if, as quite often happens, a world record-holder is left on the sidelines because he had an off day at the trials. The 'sudden-death' nature of their trials is fully understood by the American competitors and it is rigidly enforced even in cases of outstanding misfortune, such as in 1960 when their best sprinter Jeff Farrell had an emergency appendectomy a few days before the Olympic trials. Amazingly he still competed and although he had the fastest 100 metres time of the entire trials (in both heats and semi-finals) he could only finish fourth in the final and thereby lost his chance of an individual place, although he was included in the relay squad.

But this procedure has much more to commend it than its trouble-free method of selection. This type of trial allows the swimmer to prepare his season intelligently for a peak performance at a given time. It is obviously of paramount importance to the selectors that they should know which competitors can successfully achieve this under conditions of genuine competitive stress. After all, this is exactly the kind of individual they are looking for, and it was in this particular requirement that Britain's recent Olympic swimming teams were notably inadequate.

The solitary disadvantage of this system is its inflexibility in situations such as the Jeff Farrell one, but I believe that even this can be overcome. Let us suppose that we are holding trials for an Olympic Games, and therefore can select three competitors for each event. My selection policy would be as follows:

1. The first selection for the event shall be the winner of the official trial *regardless of standard of performance.*

2. The second selection for the event shall be the second swimmer in the official trial provided the 'minimum requirement' time has been achieved.

3. The third selection for the event shall be third swimmer in the official trial, provided the minimum requirement time has been achieved, unless, bearing in mind medical and other relevant considerations, the selectors feel that the consistency and *significantly faster competitive* performances during that season of some other swimmer warrants his being awarded the third position.

Minimum requirement times are necessary not so much to prevent mediocre performances from representing Britain in events in which we are weak, but more important, to show that justice is seen to be done. Without such times it would be very easy for an individual who finishes second, and is not selected, to feel that he has been victimized, but if these times are known in advance, there can be no complaints and unexpected disappointments.

I would calculate the set times from the world records for each event, as at January of that year, and add 5 per cent (or some similar percentage). I think that there are three major advantages in this method over the present system of using the finals of the previous Olympic Games. If we update the basis of our calculations by some three years, the times will obviously have much greater current relevance. Secondly, world records come closer to providing an absolute standard than a particular placing in an Olympic final, and thirdly an addition factor of 5 per cent is a genuine constant, whereas a race placing is obviously not, because of the human factor involved.

I strongly believe also that the best British swimmer in each event should go to the Olympic Games regardless of his performance. I feel that anyone who has managed to achieve such status deserves recognition and, moreover, the fact that competitive swimming is a fairly advanced sport in this country itself provides a built-in guarantee that no ludicrously poor competitor would ever represent Britain. But, in any case, why should we be ashamed of the best that we have to offer? Certainly not at the Olympic Games, whose motto is: 'The important thing is not in winning, but in taking part.'

Such a ruling would also undoubtedly strengthen Britain's longstanding weakness in the 1500 metres freestyle and men's breast-stroke by attracting more swimmers to these traditionally 'unglamorous' events.

My final comment on selection must be to point out that although I would allow a certain amount of leeway under rule 3, I remain so strongly in favour of a man-to-man encounter being the only genuine criterion of selection, that I would invoke the final clause only in exceptional situations.

The ten days in Font Romeu had clearly had the effect of 'peaking' most of us and although this was quite the reverse of what should have resulted from our altitude training in relation to the Olympic Games in October, it nevertheless had short-term benefits.

Immediately afterwards the British team performed well in Stockholm in the annual Six Nations match between Great Britain, West Germany, France, Holland, Sweden and Italy. We won handsomely and I was well satisfied with my own victory in the 100 metres freestyle in a time of 53·7 seconds, which was only 0·3 seconds slower than my previous best over the metric distance. This qualified me with half a second to spare for the trip to Mexico, and with that hurdle surmounted I felt greatly relieved that I would now be able to devote most of my energies during the following ten weeks to my architectural studies. My final exams were spread over the period from the end of April until the end of June and for that reason I had been excused the international trials at the beginning of May. I had also decided to forego the return visit to Font Romeu in June (altered at the last moment to Switzerland due to the French communications strike), although I had agreed to compete against Canada at the end of May.

It was fortunate that I had already achieved the standard for Mexico, for those few weeks of study were so physically and mentally sapping that I could not have withstood any additional pressures.

As with most students, no matter how well-intentioned, I discovered that I had miscalculated the enormous amount of academic work to be covered before the end of June. I therefore found it necessary to work sometimes for eighteen hours a day and I swam only when I could no longer bear the solitude and desk-bound inactivity which the final cramming demanded. The three or four swims which I permitted myself weekly prevented my early-season fitness from completely disappearing, but they also had a marvellously therapeutic effect on my depressed mental state. Each time I dived into the pool the water seemed to wash away my problems. But for these brief respites I doubt if I could have survived my penance as comparatively unscathed as I did.

I suppose many sportsmen derive a similar pleasure from their chosen activity, but no other sport offers such complete isolation from worldly pressures as swimming. The physically cleansing sensation of the water is an obvious factor, but more important seems to be the realization that one is in a foreign environment, divorced from normal human surroundings, and yet one's skill allows a feeling of complete confidence and freedom. Gliding would perhaps come closest to producing the effect I am trying to describe, although it is unlikely that a pilot could safely enjoy the same degree of relaxation as the expert swimmer.

In the last week of May I emerged to compete for Britain against Canada at Coventry. I had known weeks earlier, when I agreed to swim in the match, that I could not possibly be in my best condition, but the selectors had understood my position and were apparently confident that I would still be the best British representative for the 110 yards freestyle. I scarcely shared their confidence as I set out from Falkirk on the day before the match. I knew little about the form of the Canadian men. They were generally speaking not as good as their world-class girl swimmers, but I reckoned they might well have a 55-second man in the 110 yards freestyle, and that was as fast as I felt capable of producing.

I sought out Norman Sarsfield and explained that he should not expect too much of me, and found him sympathetic, but still confident that I would lick the Canadian, Dick Kastner, about whom I knew nothing. Partly for that reason and partly because I wanted to know myself exactly how much fitness my studies had cost me, I decided to go really hard in the race, and was stunned when I touched home an easy winner in 54·6 seconds, only 1·1 seconds behind my own world record. Relatively speaking, it was one of the best swims I had ever done and I was in a much happier frame of mind after the match than I had been before. My satisfaction was to be short-lived, however, for this performance later rebounded sharply on me in the only major disagreement I ever had with a senior swimming official.

The trip to Coventry came exactly half-way through my ten-week spell of work and provided, as it were, a pleasant 'mid-term' break, but immediately it was over I plunged back into my studies and did almost no swimming at all. I planned to spend the whole month of July in getting back into reasonable shape for the A.S.A. championships at the beginning of August, which would still leave me with more than two months for my final Olympic training.

As the days and nights of seemingly never-ending drawing and reading crawled past, I gradually slipped deeper and deeper into a badly-depressed state. I lost weight, became nervous, had difficulty in sleeping and was plagued with boils on my back and ulcers in my mouth. I was extremely worried also about having agreed to swim for Britain against Hungary in Budapest in the middle of July, for already by the middle of June it was apparent that I would not be in a suitable condition.

While considering whether to withdraw, I unexpectedly received an invitation to re-visit Santa Clara for the invitation meeting in the third week in July. I wrote to George Haines explaining that I wanted to accept, but that due to studies my performances would not be up to my usual standard by that time. He replied that this was of no consequence as they would enjoy having me there in any case, and he added that if I was worried about my condition, he would be delighted to have me as his guest for the whole of July.

This offer bucked me up considerably, for I knew that a few weeks of Californian sun together with unlimited training alongside Schollander and Spitz would be the ideal tonic. I immediately wrote to Norman Sarsfield and requested that I be released from the Hungarian match. I gave him a full explanation of the facts and stressed that the prime objective of a trip to California would be to recuperate generally and to get myself into better swimming shape than would be possible if I stayed at home.

I expected him to be disappointed that I would not be in the team for Budapest, but I was totally unprepared for the tone of his reply. He pointed out that the British team needed me and that if I was fit enough to compete in the United States, I was fit enough to compete in Europe. He also made much of my good swim against the Canadians in spite of my having been relatively unfit then also. His only concession was to suggest that I go to California after I had competed for Britain.

His offer of allowing me to go after the match meant that I would then have missed the Santa Clara race. I would have been delighted to do this, of course, but not unnaturally the organizers would only pay my expenses if I actually competed in the meeting. How I spent my time thereafter was a private arrangement between George Haines and myself.

My first reaction was one of amazement that the director of Olympic training, the man pledged to bring us in the best possible condition to Mexico, could have his priorities so utterly confused. Did he really believe that a run-of-the-mill international match was more important than the Olympic preparation of *any* of the swimmers under his control? Did he imagine that I would be enhancing my Olympic prospects by competing half-fit in Hungary and then darting across the world for only a few days in California?

To understand Sarsfield's attitude one must know the man, this superb organizer with a clinical, computer-like mind, inclined when making assessments of people, to label them simply 'for' or 'against' with no other categories. This was undoubtedly one of the major factors in his deserved rise from the northern provinces into the heart of the southern-dominated Amateur Swimming Association where he will doubtless do a superb job as the first professional secretary of that body. But competitive swimmers, even adult ones, are fairly straightforward individuals with few ulterior motives and they require quite different treatment. It seemed to me, however, as if I was being dictated to quite unreasonably. I remembered how I had gone for the holiday trip to Spain instead of competing in Florida, as I had wanted. I remembered how Sarsfield had forbidden me to compete in Bremen in February because *he* thought it would adversely affect my Olympic training. I remembered also how I had swum for Britain in 1963 at the request of the selectors, when I had wanted to compete in the World Student Games in Rio de Janeiro, where, as it happened, I would almost certainly have won the gold medal! All these facts were in my mind as I replied to Sarsfield in strong terms. For the record I again pointed out that there had been no question of my placing more importance on the competition in California than on swimming for Britain and again stressed that the only consideration in my mind had been to take advantage of this training opportunity which would certainly have improved my performances for Britain in the place that really mattered – Mexico City.

He returned my letter with a note saying that he could not accept it because of its tone of disrespect, but that if I insisted on sending it he would pass it on to the G.B. committee for disciplinary action.

By this time I was so sick of the whole business that I never replied to him. Sarsfield's decision had brought me to the stage where I cared little whether I swam in the Olympics or not. It seemed pointless to continue training and make other sacrifices only to be exposed to unsympathetic treatment such as I had just experienced.

Consequently I did not go to California nor to Hungary, where Britain was defeated by 155 points to 140. Ironically we still won both the team races in which I would have been competing and although the Hungarians won the individual sprint, a victory by me would not have affected the match result.

July was a difficult month for me, for it took several weeks to shake off the apathy which resulted from my altercation with the Olympic manager and the situation was aggravated because I was also having difficulty in arranging enough time in the water. I needed a great deal of bulk training and although I could train in the morning before the pool was officially open, it was impossible to swim during the day because of the hordes of school children enjoying their summer holidays. Nor was my mental approach as positive as in the past, for the thought still rankled in my mind that I could have been training under perfect conditions in California.

Towards the end of the month I decided to go to London in an effort to find the required water space in a long-course pool. This proved an abortive move, for the rather erratic environment of a friend's bachelor flat (in which I slept on a mattress on the floor), was hardly conducive to Olympic training. I found also that my unfamiliarity with the geography of London had caused me to miscalculate badly the important question of travelling between Kilburn and the National Recreational Centre at Crystal Palace. In short, I again failed to muster the amount of training which I should have been doing at that time.

Almost before I knew it, it was Nationals week at Blackpool, where I arrived in what was relatively speaking the most unfit condition of any of my seven visits to the championships. I was not at all confident of retaining my sprint title, as Tony Jarvis had done 55 seconds for the distance at the April trials, and that was not far from my 54·1-second swim (converted from metres) in the Six Nations match. There seemed little likelihood of my repeating a swim of that quality now, yet I knew that Jarvis would probably improve on his time, as most English swimmers seem to surpass themselves at the annual championships.

I kept my fitness doubts entirely to myself and decided to go flat out in the heat to see exactly what my form was. Fortunately I drew an easy heat, for the considerable distance by which I won gave the false impression that I was 'cruising'. The time of 54 seconds dead surprised and delighted me as it was only 0·5 seconds slower than my world record, which several pressmen seemed to think I was sure to improve in the final. It suited my purpose to play along with their opinions for I was keen to intimidate Jarvis if I possibly could, and I agreed (with some misgivings for I had never deceived the Press before) that I had been swimming within myself and would probably break the world record in the final!

When the Saturday evening eventually arrived and I found myself on the block looking down the stretch of water which had already brought me four world records, my mental approach to the race was totally positive and I was telling myself that I could improve my world records. Jarvis was in the next lane, but I was unaware of him till the critical final fifteen yards of the race. Until then I had swum well on technique and basic condition, but when I asked my body to maintain its effort nothing happened and at that moment Jarvis came with his typical fast finish.

I fought rather than swam the final few yards and just held on to win by 0·4 seconds in 53·9 seconds.

'So much for gamesmanship,' I thought, looking at close quarters at Jarvis's lantern-jawed features, as they gave their well-known end-of-race interpretation of agony. But the Londoner had certainly produced a first-rate performance, the best of his career in my opinion, and the manner in which he had refused to be affected by my reputation and heat swim reflected great credit on him.

I was well enough pleased with my own performance not only because of the encouraging time but also because in my final championship appearance I had managed to maintain the undefeated sequence begun in 1962.

The Olympic team was announced the following day, and it was neither a great surprise, nor a disappointment to me that I was dropped as team captain. The official reason was my failure to attend all the training weekends and international matches, but as this was due to the obviously overriding importance of career studies, I found the official explanation unacceptable. I remain convinced that my disagreement with Norman Sarsfield over the Santa Clara trip made some form of punishment inevitable, and depriving me of the captaincy seemed the best way to inflict it.

The fact that I was not particularly aggrieved did not reflect my lack of interest in the team as a whole. I simply felt that the relationship which I had built up in the six years since my first captaincy would continue whether I was officially captain or not.

The duties of a captain fall into two main categories: social and competitive. The first includes such things as attending functions, making speeches, writing letters and many other semi-administrative tasks, and in this respect I was a poor captain, for I had little flair for these things and even less liking for them.

The other responsibilities are the poolside ones, where a captain should give a lead with his competitiveness and thereby encourage his team-mates to produce that something extra. I always placed much more importance on this second aspect of captaincy and having established myself in this vein over the preceding few years, I was confident that it would need more than a change of captain to alter the direction of the team's loyalty.

The selectors had adhered rigidly to the announced selection policy except in the cases of Alan Kimber and Keith Bewley of the Southampton Swimming Club. Kimber had in fact achieved the selection time over 400 metres individual medley and Bewley had narrowly missed them in three events, but he had done more than enough to guarantee selection for a team race. The omissions were not explained by the selection committee, although Austin Rawlinson, President of the A.S.A., pointedly read out the following statement before the team was announced: 'The committee has selected this team of swimmers and divers to uphold the power and the *dignity* of youth, of our sport, and of Great Britain.' It was clear to everyone 'in the know' that the statement was an indirect reference to the conviction and fining of Kimber and Bewley for shoplifting a few weeks before the championships.

I felt sorry for them, as they seemed to have been punished far in excess of their crime, even though I had small affection for either, particularly Kimber, who seemed to me to be the one who usually led; but I could not ignore the tremendous amount of work which both boys must have done to reach their high standard of swimming, and that in itself was concrete evidence of some strength of character.

Although we were officially forbidden to comment on this matter, the team naturally discussed it amongst themselves. We could all remember minor incidents in which Kimber and Bewley had been involved while under A.S.A. jurisdiction, but none which could have prompted their non-selection for Mexico City. We were, therefore, all convinced that their conviction for

shoplifting while at home in Southampton had alone caused the
selectors to take such a strong line. We all thought that they
should have been given a stern warning about their future behaviour, but it seemed somehow almost sadistic to punish them
again in a second court for the same offence. It will not be
forgotten that Alan Kimber and Keith Bewley were not selected
for the Olympic Games, because they had pinched two pairs of
trousers from a multiple store. They needed to be helped and
not publicly dishonoured.

They both swam for Britain subsequently but were then
summarily banned from again representing England and Great
Britain, apparently *sine die*, for alleged drinking and 'skylarking'
during an international match. This might appear to vindicate
the selectors' earlier decisions in 1968, although I believe that
sympathetic handling at that time would have guaranteed their
future conduct. Be that as it may, however, I am certain that
many past international swimmers will agree with me that to
punish them for this particular crime smacks of hypocrisy. I
have never heard of an official being censured for undecorous
behaviour of that nature and yet there were times during my
career when certain of these gentlemen should most certainly
have been disciplined.

I was awakened in our hotel at 3 o'clock in the morning
before a match by a loud hammering outside my bedroom. I
rose and discovered that the noise was caused by our team
manager who had apparently locked himself in the bathroom. He eventually appeared clad only in his underpants and
smelling strongly of drink. He lurched his way into his bedroom.

I have twice seen other officials who were travelling with the
team helped to bed after drinking too much. One in fact was so
completely comatose that he had to be carried to his room. Yet
another manager was never fully sober for the whole four-day
period of one trip.

Nor did all of these incidents pass unnoticed, for there was
usually more than one senior official accompanying representa-

11a. The Hall of Fame meeting in Florida. In that weather no wonder film star Buster Crabbe and I have something to smile about

11b. Esther Williams, another former champion swimmer turned film star, chats with Olympic winner Don Roth, top American coach Doc Counsilman and myself

12. The successful British team at the World Student Games in Tokyo in 1967

tive teams, but the others seem to turn a blind eye to the behaviour of their less temperant colleagues. This was probably because travelling abroad with a team (all expenses paid of course) was one of the highly desirable perks of being a senior official. It was a privilege granted usually to a fairly select group, and provided that the 'spoils' were being fairly divided the recipients seemed to shrink from atangonizing each other unnecessarily. All the individuals described in the above episodes travelled with teams on subsequent occasions.

Having made these observations, it would be less than fair to leave the impression that this was typical 'official' behaviour. Of course, it was not, for most of those to whom teams were entrusted were reliable efficient men with whom I was proud to be associated. But it is important that the behaviour of a minority be brought into public view, for everybody inside swimming is aware of the position and too little has been said about it in the past. It is wrong for such behaviour to be condoned by silence. It is a travesty that such individuals should judge the infrequent and relatively mild indiscretions of any swimmer.

But to return to the Olympic selections: the unluckiest swimmer of all was undoubtedly David Butler of Gloucester, the British 220-yard back-stroke champion. He was the most notable victim of the lopsided selection times set by the Great Britain Committee. The standard for his event was a difficult one, yet he failed to achieve it by only 0·4 seconds. In relation to real world standards, he deserved to be selected more than most of those who were and everybody apart from the selectors seemed to realize this. No one could possibly have complained at his selection, for he was the only national senior champion not included in the team, and that in itself would have been reason enough to 'bend' the selection policy of choosing only qualified swimmers for an individual event. Moreover, a third of those who did make the team had not achieved the necessary time standards either, but were selected for team races where the aggregate time was likely to be good enough.

I

Being only a mediocre sprinter, Butler could not qualify in this manner.

It must be small consolation to Butler, but he can justly consider himself the best swimmer for many years not to have represented Britain in an Olympic Games.

XIV. Mexico City

I spent the five weeks between the championships and departure for Mexico at home in Falkirk, desperately trying to pile up the mileage which I should have done in the early summer. My training time was still limited until the end of August, due to the schoolchildren still being on holiday, but during the first two weeks in September they were back at school and I was managing to swim for more than three hours a day. In spite of these improved conditions, however, I was pleased when 15 September finally arrived and the Olympic team left Heathrow Airport for Mexico. I was looking forward to being able to do unlimited training at altitude in the month before the Games opened, and the fact that most of the swimming would be outdoor in an apparently delightful climate was a further attraction. Only another swimmer can fully appreciate the joy of warm, open-air training in comparison with the bleak, cage-like conditions which the British climate forces most competitive swimmers to endure for most of the year.

The first few days in Mexico City were spent in acclimatization, and this reprieve from training allowed us to take stock of the Olympic scene.

Our accommodation was rather cramped and lacked sufficient furniture, but the other major amenities of the Olympic Village were excellent. Norman Sarsfield did a fine job in making our quarters more comfortable and the programme of social diversions which he arranged in conjunction with willing members of the British community in Mexico was beyond praise.

Unlike many great metropolitan areas of the world the sky-line of Mexico City was not completely dominated by lofty concrete towers. Many of the new buildings had grown out-wards rather than upwards, yet there still seemed to be plenty of open space and the principal roads were wide and tree-lined. This style of planning, however, has made Mexico City the most sprawling city I have ever visited and a journey within the city limits could mean travelling several miles. On some days we spent two or three hours in coaches shuttling from one of the eleven fifty-metre training-pools to another.

The excessive travelling did not help training morale, which was as bad as the 'social' morale was good. Squad work-outs under a single coach were almost non-existent and yet this, in my opinion, is the only way in which a real team spirit can be bred. The arrival of the individual coaches of several of the swimmers caused a fragmentation of training which had a negative effect on the team as a whole. A casual observer of a British team-training session would never have concluded that the swimmers all belonged to the same team. He would have seen anything up to ten coaches, each with one or two swimmers, pursuing a quite independent training schedule.

Obviously there is a place for detailed work of this nature, but it was carried to an absurd degree in Mexico City with the result that one could not help feeling that the fact that we were all members of a British team was very secondary to individual considerations. The atmosphere was similar to that which always prevails at Blackpool during the National Championships, when understandably each individual is interested in himself. But this ought to be eliminated when a team is involved, and if it is the swimmer will surely produce a better performance.

If I had organized team training, one of the two daily train-ing sessions would have been given over to squad work, with all swimmers doing virtually the same programmes – on their own strokes of course – divided into waves of similar time ability. The second session could then have been preferably given over to more individual coaching.

Anyone watching the Americans could not have doubted that here was a single unit at work, as they swam in groups of six or eight, following each other at set intervals. Nor do I think it wrong to make the whole team do similar training. Nowadays, there are few secrets of how to prepare a swimmer for an important event, for all the world's leading coaches have written at great length on the subject and it is surprising how little they differ in their approach to the last few weeks of training. It is unlikely, therefore, that any swimmer would have been adversely affected by a competently-planned general training programme.

Our already unsatisfactory training system was further undermined by the poor team morale which it fostered. This lack of spirit caused dreadful training discipline. With few exceptions our swimmers did not work hard enough and many of them were managing to talk their coaches into allowing unnecessary rest periods, often using the altitude as an excuse. It appeared to me that Norman Sarsfield was surprisingly easy prey in this respect, for he seemed unable to differentiate between genuine training distress and 'lead-swinging', and he was far more likely to say 'Take ten minutes in the sun', than something like 'Real champions begin to swim when it hurts'.

The need for one coaching supremo was even more apparent now than during the Olympic Training Squad sessions throughout the previous year. Hamilton Bland had never attempted to impose his will upon the swimmers, and while in Mexico City he was little more than a training adjutant to Sarsfield, who persisted in trying to do the job of chief coach in addition to the managerial duties which he was performing so well (in spite of many administrative difficulties caused by the 'manana' attitude of the Mexicans).

It was against this unfortunate background that Sarsfield decided to hold a match against the Australians only a week before the Games opened. The team was unanimously against competing with anybody at that late stage, and certainly not with swimmers of the calibre of the Australians. Norman Sarsfield, however, was adamant that the match was necessary and would serve a useful purpose.

It posed awkward problems, similar to those that all of us had already experienced prior to the match with Holland at Font Romeu in April. Nobody wanted to taper for the rest yet nobody wanted to do a bad performance and perhaps be defeated by a potential rival so soon before the Games opened. In short, the contest placed unnecessary psychological strain at a critical time on a team already not too happy with itself.

We all knew that trials were necessary to select certain relay places, but the general feeling was that if it was considered absolutely necessary to have a match, then Sarsfield should have approached only those countries known to be much weaker than ourselves in order to give us a victory boost. As it was we were publicly outclassed by the Australians in the Olympic Pool in front of a fairly large crowd of swimmers, coaches and journalists, and team morale plunged even further. It was against this background that I found myself lost in the uncharacteristic weighing-up of my rivals, with which this story began.

The exuberant Mexican fans, who had proved a distant, noisy background to my open-eyed reverie, were suddenly quiet, and the ominously stirring notes of the 'Battle Hymn of the Republic' told me that Alex Jackson had not won the ladies' sprint. I was genuinely disappointed, for I had always considered her an immensely talented performer with great reserves of strength which the Olympic final might broach.

The door opened and a Mexican call-steward indicated that it was now time for us to proceed to the starting area. We moved out in single file in lane order led by Ken Walsh, then Luis Nicolao, Leonid Ilichev, Mike Wenden, Zac Zorn, myself, Mark Spitz and finally, Georgi Kulikov.

Now began the period of most intense concentration, when I tried to think of nothing but the race. Shouts of encouragement and familiar faces could make no impression on my protective shell, but on this occasion I permitted myself a glance at the scoreboard to see exactly where Alex Jackson had finished. She was placed only sixth and the Americans had taken all three medals, with Jan Henne first in 60 seconds, a time which I had believed Alex capable of in the light of her heat swim of 60·5 seconds.

In spite of my admiration for the Americans and the manner in which they always seemed to react positively to pressure, I could not help feeling a little resentful that they had already won five of the six titles competed for and that even in the notoriously fickle field of sprinting their girls had managed to beat all-comers.

I looked at the tall, shambling hulk of Zac Zorn two paces ahead of me and thought with a confidence bred from my many man-to-man victories over him, 'That's one American who won't beat me'. He would be ahead up the first, for he had the world's best starting-dive and a great pick-up, but he had never struck me as being a 'pressure' swimmer and he often faded in the latter stages.

We reached the blocks. I sat on the chair behind lane six and looked at the ballet-dancer-like physique of Spitz on my immediate left in lane seven. He looked very worried, as well he might with the possibility of four more finals ahead of him. He was one of my most dangerous opponents, for he possessed the very qualities which had deprived me of a gold medal in Tokyo: the sprinter with middle-distance stamina for the pain-racked final fifteen metres.

In lane four to my right, beyond Zorn, was the only other finalist I considered to have a chance of a gold medal, Mike Wenden. Slim-hipped but with a heavily-muscled torso, he was the most formidable opponent of all. Whoever beat him would win the gold but I was just as sure that I would join him on the rostrum.

We disrobed and on the starter's signal mounted the blocks. 'Take your marks.' I crouched, willing the far end of the pool closer. 'The last, last time. Please make it a good one.' The gun, the sudden refreshing coolness and I knew I had started well, although Zorn, as expected, was already moving away. I tried to swim as relaxed as possible without letting his waist move further away than the level of my head. At 25 metres I was slightly ahead of Spitz, but Zorn's hips were already at my head and no swimmer had ever managed that so early in the race.

At the half-way turn Spitz was still behind me, as I knew he had to be at this stage, if I were to beat him, but Zorn was now nearly a body length up and it worried me that perhaps he had picked the right time to produce a supreme effort.

I still felt good and I started to give everything after the push-off. By the 75 metres Zorn had fallen right back to me and I knew he was finished. As he faded he revealed that Wenden was well ahead and at that point I kissed the gold medal good-bye, for I knew that the Australian had the strength to hold on till the wall.

Spitz was now level with me and as I desperately tried to hold my technique in the final few metres, he moved ahead and clearly out-touched me.

I experienced scant pleasure in winning, as I thought, a bronze medal, for much of the motivation for my continued presence in international swimming had been my hopes of improving on the silver medal I had won in Tokyo. Having failed in that my actual placing seemed irrelevant provided that I had performed well enough to do justice to my country and to myself.

With feelings which I can describe only as being rather neutral, I was gathering up my track-suit and bathrobe when I overheard George Haines congratulating Spitz on his bronze medal. A glance along the other lanes confirmed that Walsh, surrounded by a little group of photographers, must have slipped into second place. This was remarkable, for Walsh had barely qualified for the semi-finals and had been second lowest into the final. Before the final even his own team had written him off as a medal prospect.

The disappointment at missing the bronze medal, although in itself not overwhelming, was sufficient to trigger off for the first time memories of Tokyo. My spirits sank and I trudged off along the poolside past the British team benches where everyone looked as low as I felt, for it now seemed certain then that our team would return empty-handed to Britain.

Wenden's time was a magnificent 52·2 seconds, which clipped 0·4 seconds off the previous world record. The brilliance of his performance actually cheered me up considerably, for I realized that I could never have achieved such a time no matter how smoothly my training had gone in the previous four months.

Walsh was second in 52·8 seconds, Spitz third in 53·0 seconds, and myself fourth in 53·5 seconds, which was 0·1 second slower than my best metric swim.

I felt relieved to be out of the competitive rat-race, for I knew I could never accept second-rate status and Wenden's swim had set a distinctly higher standard than I or anyone else had ever attained. But he had achieved it only after probably the most strenuous period of organized training ever undergone by a group of athletes. In the twelve weeks before the Games the Australians had each covered 500 miles in training under one coach, and this brought them much greater success than their pre-Olympic world rankings had indicated.

Immediately after the race I went off to a secluded part of the changing-room in order to dress leisurely, and quietly mull over the thoughts that flooded my mind after my final race. I was still there thirty minutes later, when a rather flustered Norman Sarsfield appeared with the news that I had almost been disqualified for failing to report for a urine test. I would have to go at once.

It seemed rather pointless in my case, but off I went and on entering the medical room I was surprised to find a sheepish-looking Mark Spitz still there clasping a glass of water. He had been unable to muster the required specimen and was now on his fourth glass of water, patiently waiting to prove that he had not been drugged and could therefore keep his bronze medal!

I complied with the regulations and left the sad-eyed Spitz unamused by my comment that I hoped he made it before the medical room was taken over by the swimmers from the next ladies' final, which he well knew was the following evening!

XV. Mexico in Retrospect

Having started badly for Britain, the Mexico Games continued in much the same vein and in many respects they proved to be an even bigger disaster to our swimming prestige than the Tokyo Games had been four years earlier. It was not that the members of the 1968 team performed less well than their 1964 counterparts, for the Mexico results were in general rather better than those achieved in 1964. But when one also takes into consideration the far greater amounts of time and money that were lavished on the 1968 squad, then the extent of its failure is shown much more realistically.

There is no doubt we should have done much better than we did. This is not to say that our swimmers could reasonably have been expected to return with a pocket-full of medals, for although medals may be the ultimate and most obvious yardstick of Olympic success they are not by any means the only one. In fact, medals can even give a false impression of success, if by 'success' we mean the achievement of the optimum performance of which an individual is capable. Many brilliant sportsmen owe their success largely to great natural talent which they do not need to exploit fully in order to stay ahead of the field. While at the other end of the spectrum there are many sportsmen, with scant natural gifts, who drive themselves through sheer hard work and determination to a level of performance beyond what could naturally be expected of them. They are as much the heroes of the sporting world and of most other fields of human endeavour as the fortunate few who are seen to carry off the prizes. It is in these terms rather than in medals that the most realistic stamp of Olympic success is represented.

In the sports which are governed by the absolute measurements of time, weight or distance, therefore, any athlete who produces a personal best performance can be said to be successful, for he has risen to the real challenge which the Olympic Games present to sportsmen throughout the world, namely so to arrange their physical and mental capabilities that they can produce their best when it is required. It was in this crucial requirement of the competitive athlete that Britain's swimmers failed in the last two Olympic Games.

In Mexico the British team never recovered from the two hefty blows to their principal medal hopes so early in the Olympic programme. As disappointment followed disappointment morale plummeted. The situation was not helped by Norman Sarsfield's continued assumption of the roles of chief coach and team manager, for the administrative and communication failings of the Mexicans made the latter job more than enough for one man. It was a combination of these factors which caused a major disagreement between Norman Sarsfield and several of the senior members of the team.

Sarsfield had been advising us of the times likely to be required for safe qualification into the semi-finals, but experience had taught us that these were best ignored. In the case of the men's 100 metres back-crawl, however, our first string, Roddy Jones, was told by Sarsfield that there were three semi-finals. Jones swam well within himself and would have qualified easily for the first twenty-four places, but he was shocked to find afterwards that there were only two semi-finals and that he was out.

Sarsfield's explanation was that the official circular which was sent to all team managers two days earlier must have been stolen from his letter-box. In spite of his disappointment Jones was willing to accept this, but he was extremely hurt when he was informed that on the basis of his heat swim (about two seconds slower than his usual performance) he would not be selected for the medley team race, in which Neil Jackson would do the back-stroke leg.

All the swimmers involved, including Martyn Woodroffe, who stood to lose his place as a result of Jackson's new British 100 metres butterfly record in Mexico City, agreed that Jones should be selected, as he had always beaten Jackson on back-stroke and had led off the team for all their previous best performances.

On behalf of the team Tony Jarvis requested that Jones be selected, but this was refused.

That evening several of the men swimmers had a meeting in our quarters and there was unanimous agreement that an injustice had been done to Jones. We also felt that if he were not selected we would be disinclined to compete in the event.

Having failed with our direct approach to Sarsfield we 'leaked' the story to a reporter, who did a short but accurate piece for television that same night. The repercussions were immediate. Early next morning Sarsfield received calls from the Press and the A.S.A. in London, asking for an explanation of the swimmers' 'mutiny'. He categorically denied that there had been any meeting of swimmers, nor was there any question of a mutiny. He was wrong, of course, on the first point, although he did not know it, but right on the second, for although we were very angry, all the swimmers involved fully intended to give their best for Britain when the time came, no matter who was selected to swim. We merely wanted to draw attention to what we considered an unjust team selection.

Sarsfield was both furious and deeply hurt and, although we considered our action justified, it was nevertheless impossible not to feel sorry for him, for we were all well aware of his unselfish dedication to Olympic preparations throughout the year before the Games. He was now obviously utterly dejected at the realization that he had lost the support of a large section of the team.

He rallied himself, however, refused to accept that a meeting had taken place and insisted that there was a spy in the camp, whom he would 'gladly punch on the nose'. He also banned all reporters of Independent Television from talking to members of the British team, on the grounds that they had broadcast an unauthenticated story. Unfortunately, however, he stuck to his guns on the team race selection, although he did offer Roddy Jones an unpaced time trial, which Jones was right to refuse.

In a similar situation in the Tokyo Olympics, the Americans used a different approach. One of their star performers, Roy Saari, had produced a number of below-form swims during the Games and his earlier selection for the 200 metres freestyle team race was in jeopardy. The coaches *consulted the swimmers involved* and *together* they agreed that Saari's past record of consistency warranted his retention. Saari vindicated their confidence in him by producing his best performance of the Games, as the Americans won the gold medal in a world record time.

In Mexico, Britain's team failed to qualify for the final, but if Jones had swum his *average* time and Jackson had switched to butterfly with the same time he had done earlier in the week, the team would have improved about two seconds, and been one of the last eight countries in the final.

As the competitions continued, the twice-daily visits to the Olympic Pool developed into a kind of penance for us. It was unnerving to watch the events slip by as we waited for the final day when it seemed inevitable that we would be branded the only British swimming team in the history of the Olympic Games to return home without a single medal.

Sarsfield's patience with the team was fast running out, and when Martyn Woodroffe failed to reach his third final, he turned away with a mildly derogatory comment about Welshmen. Jones overheard the remark and was incensed enough to bring it up later in the evening when several of the team were talking together. During the ensuing discussion it was decided that so much had gone wrong in so many aspects of the preparations for the Olympics that our feelings should be made known officially to the A.S.A. We therefore composed a letter which was sent from Mexico to Alderman Harold Fern, who had for nearly fifty years been secretary of the A.S.A. and was also chairman of the Great Britain Committee, and to Austin Rawlinson, President of the A.S.A. and secretary of the G.B. Committee. Norman Sarsfield also received the letter.

A copy was retained for reference. I reproduce its text:

> Olympic Village,
> Mexico,
> 27 October 1968

Dear

The undersigned senior members of the Great Britain Olympic Swimming Team feel that in the light of the comparative lack of success of the team at the recent Olympic Games, we should present the following observations:

1. *Pre-competition*

a. There existed a complete lack of confidence in the two appointed coaches, who were both unproven and lacking in practical experience, especially at such a high level.

b. There was little discipline during training sessions. Indeed, individual swimmers were allowed to train as they pleased. There was no squad work of the type practised by the British team in previous major competitions, and this led to an absence of the team spirit which normally results from such training.

c. The senior team coach was allowed to go on holiday for two days at a crucial time in our preparation, namely two weeks before the commencement of the Games.

d. We feel that the team manager should confine himself to administrative duties, and should not interfere with coaching.

2. *Competitive Period*

a. On several occasions the team manager wrongly advised team members on times necessary to qualify for semi-finals.

b. There was a major administrative blunder in the relation to the number of semi-finals for the Men's 100 Metres Backstroke, which acutely affected Roddy Jones's chances of progressing to the semi-finals.

c. Swimmers who swam below form were unsympathetically handled.

d. There appeared to be a lack of interest on the part of the team manager and coaches in the Olympic swimming generally. When no team member was competing, they were not in attendance at the pool, and opportunities of improving our knowledge of world swimming were lost.

e. On one occasion the chief coach attended the athletics stadium when British swimmers were actually competing. We offer these points completely without malice, in the hope that some constructive propositions will emerge, to the future benefit of British teams.

We wish to thank Norman Sarsfield for his administration and social arrangements prior to the Games, and Mrs Toms for her excellent work as Team Chaperone. Alan Hime and Roger Eady were a great help, but much greater use could have been made of their abilities. Finally, we feel that the selection of team captain should be made by the team members.

signed:

It was signed by all the men swimmers except Ray Terrell, whom we considered too young to become involved in case there might be repercussions, and Tony Jarvis.

cc. Alderman H. E. Fern, C.B.E., J.P.
A. Rawlinson, Esq, M.B.E.
N. W. Sarsfield, Esq, M.C.

The text is self-explanatory except for the references to Alan Hime and Roger Eady, and the final comment about the selection of a team captain.

Hime was the very experienced coach of several of the swimmers in the team. He was taken to Mexico by the A.S.A. to assist his own swimmers, although he had no official position. Eady was the brilliant young coach of Martyn Woodroffe. He travelled independently to Mexico and joined the British training sessions, working exclusively with Woodroffe.

13a. Training at Crystal Palace. Olympic team-mate Neil Jackson is in the water

13b. Another action shot which shows how I could breathe to both sides (c.f. plate 9b). It is important for front-crawlers to be able to do this comfortably

14. The 100 metres line-up at the Six Nations match in Dortmund in 1967. This gives a good impression of how I tried to concentrate and relax immediately before a start

We included the comment about the selection of a team captain because the team in general was disappointed at the competitive showing and attitude of Tony Jarvis. Although he did well administratively, he gave little lead in dedicated training; in his races he gave the impression of being beaten before he started, and consequently his performances were very far below his best.

When our comments were considered by the G.B. Committee some weeks after the Games, they declared that no action was to be taken. If by that they meant that no action was to be taken against any individual, then I would heartily agree, for as we hoped to make clear in the letter, our criticisms were not intended to indict anyone. But if by 'no action' they mean that our observations are to be ignored, then I am certain that no British team will ever perform well in international competitions similar to the Olympic Games. No matter how well prepared the swimmers may be beforehand, if they have no confidence in their officials in the vital pre-competitive period, the team's morale must wane and without that success is impossible.

After my return from Mexico, Denis Howell, the Minister for Sport, invited me to travel to London to discuss the contents of the letter and also to put forward any recommendations which I might have developed during my several years in international swimming. I suggested that it would be valuable to hear the views of a girl swimmer also, and as a result Alex Jackson also went to the meeting.

Mr Howell seemed sympathetic to the points which we raised, and although he made it quite clear that he could give no guarantee to implement our suggestions his concern about our lack of success in Mexico and his desire to help were obviously genuine. He did surprise me, however, by clearly being out of sympathy with Bert Kinnear's resignation a year before the Olympics. In spite of Kinnear's reasons for his action (the appointment of an unqualified National Technical Officer), Howell thought he should have continued until the Olympics were over.

K

My swimming memories of Mexico are not all unpleasant, however, and I am proud that one of the bravest performances of the entire Games should have come from a British swimmer.

Martyn Woodroffe failed to reach the finals of the 200 and 400 metres individual medleys and the 100 metres butterfly, with performances below what we had come to expect of him, and when he qualified for the 200 metres butterfly as the second slowest man in the final, it seemed even to his team-mates that he had achieved his limit. But we reckoned without his determination and refusal to accept defeat. The manner in which he won his silver medal by clinging to and almost defeating the American gold medallist Carl Robie was worthy of the highest praise.

In this swim Woodroffe epitomized everything that is admirable in athletic competition and in the Olympic Games themselves. He is definitely not a 'natural', he was not heavily sponsored by the State or by a university, and he coached himself until a year before the Olympics, yet by sheer hard work and will-power he managed to drive himself far beyond his own previous limits. His was one of the success stories of the Games.

That same final of the 200 metres butterfly highlighted one of the great failures of the Games, when the American wonder-boy Mark Spitz staggered into last place, in a time some eight seconds slower than his own world record. Spitz had come to Mexico with an apparently reasonable chance of winning three individual and three team-race gold medals. The pressure proved too much for him, however, and having failed to win the freestyle sprint and in particular the butterfly sprint, for which he also held the world record, he approached the 200 metres butterfly psychologically defeated already.

If he had had Woodroffe's spirit allied with his own ability, the other seven finalists would not have been at the races, but unlike Woodroffe, Spitz seemed unable to shake off the disappointment of his previous swims. He set off at a ridiculously fast pace as if to show everyone what he could really do and led easily at fifty metres. After the first turn he virtually collapsed and was obviously out of the race by the seventy-metre mark.

Even on a bad off-day Spitz would have been up with the leaders at the end, and he must have known this, but clearly he thought in terms of gold or nothing. His psychological state made the gold doubtful, so I believe he set out for a 'nothing' so disastrous that it would seem obvious that something was wrong with him.

My interpretation of Spitz's swimming may appear over-harsh, but I give it, not to belittle an extremely gifted swimmer, but more to show how the pressures of the Olympic Games can undermine the greatest talents.

Many months after this incident, I read that George Haines had dropped Spitz from the Santa Clara club for refusing to compete for them in the national club championships.

XVI. The Money Question

When I decided in the late 1950s that swimming was to be my major sport, I suppose like most schoolboys I hoped that some day it would bring me fame, but never was there any thought that success could also bring fortune. Swimming was then, and still is, one of the most amateur of all sports, with strict national and international governing bodies, and the most that the champion could hope for was a few years of interesting travel with all expenses paid. In fact it was accepted by myself and my parents that, no matter how successful I might become, it would cost time, effort and money to reach international status.

And so it proved. While most of my student friends took vacation work to supplement their grants, I could never do so, because of the demands of training and the numbers of days off required for major swimming events. I never complained about this situation, for I loved swimming and there were many compensations which made the loss of a few pounds seem unimportant.

It was only when I began to travel a great deal during the sixties that I realized that many countries, sports associations and individuals were playing the amateur game with a quite different set of rules from the ones I was used to.

Two of my earliest trips were to East Germany and Hungary, and it was clear from my first conversations with members of these teams that they were considered very special people within the social structure of the State.

The East Germans had little to say for themselves, but the

Hungarians were much more forthcoming and I learnt that all their best sportsmen were allowed by the State to leave their employment at certain times each day for training, and for as many days or weeks as was necessary for matches or special team training. All absences, of course, were on full pay. In addition to that, they had priority in jobs and housing, were entitled to travel free on public transport and had meal vouchers which enabled them to eat without charge in the State restaurants.

Such a system puts too great a responsibility on the individual, and personally I would hate to be in a position where I felt I had to do well because the rest of my society had indulged me. From that point of view, therefore, I had no envy of the Communist system, but it did strike me that we in Britain habitually went too far in the other direction, so that not only did some of our sportsmen not receive broken-time payment for wages lost, but some even lost their jobs by accepting invitations to represent their country.

The 1962 Commonwealth Games in Perth, Australia, presented me with another significant indication of how the amateur code was being flaunted. At these Games I came in contact for the first time with many British sportsmen, including one leading English athlete who had a considerable international reputation. He had heard about my winning the silver medal and he congratulated me with the words, 'You'll be in the money now with all the invitations.'

I imagined he was talking metaphorically and I answered simply that I was indeed looking forward to as much travelling as I could. He then asked how much a star swimmer might be paid at an invitation gala. I answered that I had never received more than a hair-brush, or pen-and-pencil set, nor had I ever heard of a swimmer being offered money. He seemed genuinely surprised, but would not be drawn when I questioned him about such payments in athletics, although he made it quite clear that they existed.

It was not till two years later, by which time I was a fully-established member of the international sporting 'jet-set', that I became friendly enough with a number of British athletes to discover at first hand what had been hinted at in Perth. Several have admitted to me, on more than one occasion, that they received payments of as much as £100 for competing in invitation meetings in Europe (often in Scandinavia) and similar amounts for appearing at the annual sports of large commercial corporations in this country. In both situations they were crowd-pullers – a fact which the organizers were willing to recognize – in the most obvious fashion.

One English athlete, who was a household word at his peak a few years ago, is reputed to have earned £5,000 (tax-free of course!) in a single year, but there are many others who still make useful sums in violation of the amateur code.

It is impossible for a swimmer to 'cash in' on his reputation in this manner, because the limited size of swimming stadia, particularly in this country, makes it impossible to take large sums of money at the gate. At one European international invitation meeting, however, I saw a swimmer ask for and receive expenses of £100 from the treasurer of the commercial organization which was sponsoring the show. As he lived closer to the venue than any other swimmer in the event, it seemed a disproportionately high figure. When I asked for my own expenses, the same official seemed mildly amused by my very reasonable figure and inquired if I was certain that there was nothing I could add to 'fatten it a little'.

Not unnaturally I wanted to increase my claim, but at the back of my mind I feared that news of these expenses might filter back to the A.S.A., and being unprepared for his generous attitude I felt I would be unable to justify an excessive amount to my home association. I declined the offer, but promised myself to be on the look-out for similar opportunities in the future. As it turned out, they never arose.

The point has now been reached in international sport when there are so many flagrant violations of the amateur code that there is only one way of legitimizing the situation in a manner which is fair to all sportsmen. This is the elimination of the distinction between the amateur and the professional. Each sport has its own amateur definition and these definitions fluctuate from the strict, as in swimming, to the permissive, as in show-jumping. Yet most of the world's popular sports are featured in the Olympic Games, which themselves demand the strictest forms of amateurism, and it is therefore at this highest level of sport that the situation becomes most absurd.

The unashamed advertising of ski equipment and track-shoes, athletes actually representing commercial concerns during the Games, other sportsmen signing professional contracts before they have finished competing, are but a few of the many ways in which professionalism is rife at the world's major sports festival; but the solution does not lie in making the rules of participation even stricter, as purists suggest, for the simple reason that standards in all sports have risen so much that it is now virtually a full-time job to prepare oneself for competiton at that level. Stricter regulations would merely put the clock back fifty years, when only the privileged few could afford to take part in sport.

My own sport might appear to disprove this theory, as many of the world's outstanding swimmers are teenagers who are genuinely amateur by even the strictest definition. But they are champions not because they arc young, but because, being young, they are still at school and therefore have fewer responsibilities and more time for training. I know of many swimmers and other amateur sportsmen who are forced to abandon competition, not because they want to, but because domestic and career responsibilities preclude their continued participation without any financial return. I am certain that Communist sportsmen, generally speaking, have much longer careers than their Western counterparts because they can compete and consolidate their careers at the same time.

I am not under any circumstances suggesting a Communist-type system – quite the reverse. Under that system the State is the sportsman's patron, but I would like the individual himself to be his own provider, though obviously he must be permitted to reap his harvest as best he may.

Doubtless these words will seem a heresy to many, who will see in them the disruption of the established amateur sports associations and total commercialization of the Olympic Games. I believe that the adoption of these suggestions would only nominally affect the former, and might save the latter from falling into disrepute.

The Table Tennis Association offers the precedent on which I base my opinions. That sport is 'open' and yet an over-whelming majority of competitive table-tennis players are wholly amateur. Perhaps two or three of the best players earn their entire living through sponsorship and advertising, but most of the leading players have separate full-time jobs which they merely subsidize from playing and coaching earnings. The significant factors are that these players are able to stay in the game much longer without losing financially, and also that the Table Tennis Association is able to operate in exactly the same way as the Amateur Athletic Association, the Amateur Swim-ming Association, and other amateur bodies.

The table-tennis players, Denis Neale and Chester Barnes, have been having a battle recently, each desperate to prove himself England's 'number one', knowing that his earnings are in direct proportion to his ranking. Their play has improved with their rivalry, England has benefited in international matches, and the Table Tennis Association has also profited by additional revenue and publicity for the sport. This inter-dependence of the individual and the association is thoroughly healthy.

The situation in swimming and in other similarly amateur sports is very different for the outstanding performer. Far from helping him financially, his star status is a financial burden, for reasons less obvious than the well-known one of lost earnings. The 'star' in any sphere has a certain position in the public eye and whether he wants to or not, it is going to cost him money to live up to that position. I myself had to buy more and better clothes than I would otherwise have needed and I had a host of expenses which no normal student would have had.

As a 'personality' I was regularly invited to charity social functions, where I rubbed shoulders with people who had a great deal more money than myself. Such gatherings were often a little embarrassing for me in that I had to be very careful about when I offered to buy a round of drinks for my immediate fellow guests: a mis-reading of the situation could easily set me back a month's pocket money!

On one occasion, I was asked to pay nine pounds customs duty on a watch I had won as a prize in Switzerland. I did not have enough money, so the watch had to stay at the customs for a few weeks until I could 'bail' it out.

Another time I was asked to be a judge in the Miss England competition, and although the organizers were only too willing to pay me the same substantial fee as the other judges, I could not accept it. In fact the affair cost me money, because the invitation came when I was away from home and I had to hire a dinner-jacket in order to be suitably dressed.

However, I am not complaining about being short of money. The irksome part for me was always the realization that I was bound by a code of amateurism which almost all other sportsmen ignored. Would it have been so wrong for me to appear in a television commercial saying I liked milk or some other product which I enjoy? Why should I not have modelled sweaters or track-suits, or after-shave lotion, or even men's underwear (for which I did receive a firm offer!). Such things do not seem to have affected George Best's playing ability, or Manchester United's drawing power!

As it was, I could not have survived many of the financial demands which my star status imposed upon me had it not been for the great generosity of a wealthy retired headmaster in the Highlands of Scotland, who was my patron throughout my entire career.

Whenever I have discussed such matters with swimming officials they have always raised the nonsensical objection that it would be impossible to run the Association if swimmers wanted money for competing, a situation which they should know would never arise. Are they not merely trying to resist the possible erosion of their power over swimmers? It cannot be a genuine desire to cling to amateurism, for it has long been a practice to pay cash honoraria to officials, and more recently other officials have been paid four-figure salaries for the arrangement of television coverage.

I am wholly in favour of this. Many officials work long and hard for swimming and they deserve any recompense which the Association may wish to make out of its own coffers. Surely, therefore, it is not unreasonable that they should alter their amateur definition, so that swimmers can also earn something, particularly when the money would *not* be coming from the Association's finances?

There is only one worthwhile objection to the changes I am advocating, namely that the International Olympic Committee might not accept swimmers under such conditions. I say 'might not' because I am staggered by what they have already accepted in the case of show-jumping. These 'amateur' sportsmen actually compete for cash prizes and I read recently that one British show-jumper is expected to earn £15,000 in 1970. Some amateur!

The key to the problem is held by one man, Avery Brundage, the President of the I.O.C. He describes the laws of amateurism as being immutable, which would be fine if society had not changed in the past fifty years, and more importantly, if the I.O.C. itself had been able to implement its own 'immutable' regulations efficiently, so that all competitors were indeed of the same status. This it has manifestly failed to do and any organization which is a living sham must inevitably become a dying one.

But there is still a way in which the Olympic Games can show the sporting world a magnificent example, as indeed the Ancient Games did many centuries ago. It was customary in those days to have a truce on all warfare, so that athletes and spectators could travel safely and in a spirit of peace to Mount Olympus. The I.O.C. should relax its regulations on amateurism, but should place a total and stringent ban on any kind of advertising during the Games: a truce as it were on the commercial warfare of modern society. The character of the Games would not change at all, for the competitors would still be drawn from the same sources as before. Competitors from sports rooted in professionalism, such as cycling and boxing, although eligible, would almost certainly not wish to take part, because they would normally be unwilling to jeopardize their professional status without a guaranteed financial return. If they did participate, however, it would be a victory for Olympic ideals, because it would prove that their motives were altruistic.

Probably Mr Brundage would dislike my views intensely, but in my opinion they would lead to an honest atmosphere at future Olympic Games, something which has been notably absent in recent years.

XVII. Television and the Press

Before the widespread television coverage of sports began in the mid-1950s, swimming had been very much a backwater in terms of spectator following. Many people swam as a recreation, but dingy, out-of-date pools with little spectator accommodation and the lack of large outdoor stadia, made impracticable by our climate, caused the competitive side of the sport to be virtually unknown to the general public. Only the week-long A.S.A. championships received any national publicity in the Press, and as the four domestic associations consistently staggered from one financial crisis to another, international matches which would have generated further publicity almost always proved too costly to be undertaken.

Nowadays, however, competitive swimming has a massive public following through television, and the A.S.A. of England has achieved the status of being the nation's richest amateur sports body, with assets approaching £150,000. Swimmers themselves have great incentives to train in that there are numerous international matches and foreign trips throughout the year, and they know also that, if they are successful, they could become national sports personalities of a status previously reserved for footballers and cricketers.

Although more than one factor was involved in the transformation of the sport from 1955 onwards, there is no doubt that the major one was sponsorship by television, and in particular by BBC television. I myself, possibly more than any other swimmer, benefited from the new-found affluence of and public popularity for the sport; even so there are areas where the present system of television coverage seems to demand improvement.

Having had one season off during my career and having been retired now for more than a year, I have seen enough televised swimming to say that the presentation seems to be perfectly adequate, whether done by the BBC, or by the ITV companies which came into the field seriously in 1964, some ten years after the Corporation. Originally I did have reservations about certain commentaries, but I quickly changed my mind after trying to do the job myself! It is easy to criticize when sitting comfortably in one's own front room with no distractions, but it is a different matter when one is at the venue, surrounded by a noisy crowd, and most distracting of all, wearing headphones through which is passing a constant flow of instructions to the several cameramen, commentators, floor managers, and other assistants. Only a few of the instructions are meant for the commentator, yet he is expected to decipher them while continuing to talk! After several near-disasters on my part, it is now a source of awe to me that commentators can talk at all, let alone sensibly!

From the point of view of the swimmers, however, there have always been three major criticisms of television coverage. The first concerns the period immediately before the start of a race. This is a harrowing time for all competitors and they will want to avoid even the slightest annoyance. Yet many times they are asked to remove their track-suits for the start and then told there will be two minutes delay. Apart from the minor discomfort of having to put the garments on again, there is also the more important question of loss of body heat, and, as I know from bitter experience, most British swimming-pools, even the modern ones, are draughty and rather cold. Most swimmers understand that delays can happen in the timings of a live transmission, but they feel that they should not be asked to strip for the race until the live link-up has been made. Since the competitors in an average race line-up can remove their suits and prepare for the race in about thirty seconds, it seems a small concession to make to good relations.

The other two complaints are connected with the contractual system now in operation in Britain. Since the beginning of televised swimming, the BBC has had separate exclusive contracts with the swimming associations of Scotland and England, but in 1964 the Welsh A.S.A. and ITV signed an exclusive agreement, which was renewed last year. No athlete aims to be in good competitive condition for twelve months of the year, nor does he want to be publicly defeated. A conflict of interests is therefore inevitable between the swimmer, the associations, and the broadcasting companies. It is the 'name' performer who suffers most in this situation, for he is the one the companies want on their programme and the public want to see, yet he is the one who needs the rest most and who has most to lose from competing when not in proper condition. On many occasions international swimmers have excused themselves from competing in a particular match because they felt they would not do themselves justice. Often they were still the fastest selection, even though not in tip-top condition, and their non-appearance usually incurred the criticism of the organizing officials, many of whom place more importance on the result of an insignificant and usually contrived match than on the pride of performance which may have driven the swimmer to international honours. There is, however, a solution to this and as with most problems it lies in compromise.

The months of November, December and January should be completely free of televised competitions, and any matches in the months immediately before and after that period should be over distances and events which are not officially recognized. If the emphasis were on shorter rather than longer distances the result would certainly be exciting, closely-fought-out races, which would make excellent viewing. And what is even more important, the competitions would be fun for the swimmers, something which out-of-season matches have never been.

My third complaint raises far more important issues than

either of the earlier ones. It concerns the power wielded by the
A.S.A., and to a lesser extent by the S.A.S.A., to prevent their
swimmers from appearing in matches televised by ITV. There
were two examples of this during my own career that shocked
me. A few years ago the British Universities Swimming Championships were to be held at the National Recreation Centre in
London. The BBC had shown no interest in televising them, so
ITV offered the Universities Board a large fee for the rights to
the competitions. At that time the Universities were, as usual,
short of money and were in fact desperately trying to raise
capital to send an all-sports team to the World Student Games.
They were therefore delighted to accept ITV's offer. The A.S.A.,
however, made it clear that no English swimmers would be
given permission to appear on Independent Television. As ninety
per cent of the competitors were English, it was obvious that
the championships could not go on without them, and the
swimmers themselves were not going to risk suspension in order
to compete. The result was that there was no television, and
the Universities lost a great deal of money which they badly
needed.

The second episode was in August 1965 when the Cardiff
Corporation had arranged an impressive international invitation gala. An extremely powerful team of American swimmers,
including several world record-holders, had accepted invitations and many British swimmers had received personal invitations (a perfectly correct procedure) to take part.

This was a marvellous opportunity to see and compete against
some of the world's best swimmers, and most of the invited
British swimmers were keen to take part, but again the A.S.A.
made it clear that no English swimmer would be given permission to appear as the gala was being televised by ITV. It
seemed that this show-piece event would not take place, but
after ITV offered the BBC half of the two-day coverage the
deadlock was resolved and all the swimmers had permission to
compete.

Two points need examination. Is it right that any sports body should have the power to prevent a British *amateur* sportsman from taking part in any official competition in Britain? And secondly, is it right that a broadcasting organization should apparently be able to influence decisions affecting individual performers within a particular sport?

But the matter which disturbs me most in televised swimming is the manner in which Scotland has been very much the poor relation of the three major British associations. The S.A.S.A. has maintained its allegiance to the BBC throughout the years, and although the exact financial details of its contract are officially known only to two men (similarly with the A.S.A. contract), the continuing poverty of Scottish swimming suggests that the S.A.S.A. may have been sold short.

Scottish swimming throughout the 1950s had a significance far in excess of its size in relation to England and Wales, but in recent years it lurched to a poor third. The core of the problem lay in a lack of money which caused a lack of incentive in the swimmers. Most young swimmers look for a little more than the honour of representing their country as reward for their labours. But the means of representing their country must exist in the form of sufficient international matches at which to set their sights. Apart from the annual Bologna Trophy match and the Celtic International (v. Wales and v. Ireland) the S.A.S.A. offered its swimmers few other international matches for some ten years. The recent difficulties of Scottish swimming are the direct result of this, yet it need never have happened had a more realistic television contract been negotiated with one of the broadcasting companies.

This is not meant, however, as any criticism of the BBC. Rather it is a criticism of the officials concerned, who accepted a contract which led to a Scottish decline, and who twice apparently turned down ITV offers similar to the one accepted, with stunning success, by the Welsh A.S.A. The loss cost Scottish swimming a four-figure sum to be used exclusively for training, plus the capability of mounting each year some five international matches and several local events, and, most damaging

15. The Olympic team outside our quarters in Mexico City (1968)

16. The other side of my life. I burn the midnight oil in preparation for exams

of all, it cost the enthusiastic support of many swimmers, coaches and officials.

The situation is rapidly improving, however, now that the direction of training in Scotland is in the youthful and competent hands of the new National Technical Officer, John Hogg and also Hamilton Smith, who formerly held the same position with the A.S.A.

In general, however, the benefits brought by television to British swimming as a whole vastly outweigh these criticisms. Television made the public aware for the first time of the personalities in the sport as they actually computed, and the Press quickly followed the trend by helping to build them into national figures. My many friends on the sports benches might object to my contention that they 'followed' television in promoting personalities. It is true, of course, that they were writing up swimming before television came on the scene, but as I have said before, swimming in the early days had minute coverage in comparison to football and cricket, and it was impossible for even the most sympathetic sportswriter consistently to inject swimming reportage with the kind of personalities which a sport must have to survive in the forefront of public popularity.

Having said that, I must pay tribute to the informed manner in which swimming is reported in this country. Only on one occasion in my career did I feel that I personally might have had more sympathetic consideration, but in retrospect I can see that even that was a single bitter drop in an ocean of encouragement. I know most swimming writers in Britain by their Christian name, and most other international swimmers can say likewise, since these Pressmen are individuals who really care about the sport. They played a particularly important role in consistently supporting swimmers in their many brushes with officialdom, when the swimmers themselves were often too young to speak for themselves. Some British swimming officials have, I think, a justifiable reputation for treating their young internationals too much like children. Fifteen- and sixteen-year-olds are, indeed, still children, but when they have driven themselves

L

to the top of a very demanding sport, they should be handled in a rather more adult manner than the normal product of that age group. It was in this admittedly difficult area of official/swimmer relationships that difficulties have arisen over the years, and as often as not it was to the approachable members of the Press that the aggrieved young swimmer turned.

This brought about many disagreements between the Press and officials, one of which was serious enough to cause the Great Britain Committee to produce one of its most unworkable edicts, forbidding any swimmer on a British team to talk to a member of the Press unless a team official was present. This ban came into operation from the time of team assembly until dispersal after a match.

The result of this decision was to instil a new tension into every international event. The swimmers ignored the ban *en masse*, but most made a diplomatic pretence of obeying it, and this placed an unnecessary strain on them.

My own view of the whole question of reportage may be extreme but as the great film-maker, Sam Goldwyn, is said to have remarked, 'There's no such thing as scandal, just publicity.' Like all sports, competitive swimming relies on public interest and patronage to survive. Without personalities and interesting reportage beyond the mere results of a contest, that interest will wane and we will be back in the bad old days when swimming received a few column inches twice a year. If individuals and situations are painted slightly larger than life in the popular press it serves only to heighten public awareness of the sport; and this is surely to the good. Obviously there is a line which must not be crossed, but I have never known an occasion when a swimming-journalist has brought the sport into disrepute, and, knowing them as I do, I cannot envisage such a situation arising.

XVIII. Home and Dry

The retired international sportsman has many problems to face, the most obvious of which may well be an alarming increase in body weight, twenty pounds of which is my own constant reminder that an always healthy appetite has not yet managed to adjust to my present life of comparative inactivity! But the aftermath of a first-class sporting career can cause more serious problems, which often increase in direct proportion to the talent and success of the performer in question. Broadly speaking, I am referring to psychological difficulties on the one hand, and to career difficulties on the other.

I have always thought that most people who take up sports *seriously* do so as a means of boosting their self-confidence. They want to excel and they want to be seen to excel. While their career is successful, they are satisfying the needs of their ego, and they are therefore content. But there is one insidious aspect of a sporting talent in that, although it can raise an individual to the heights at an early age, it inevitably vanishes, as physical power begins to wane, leaving someone who is still young and often emotionally and intellectually immature, to face the daunting prospect of a life of anti-climax. One needs cast only a cursory glance over the biographies of many outstanding sportsmen to realize how frequently a successful career has been followed by an unhappy retirement. It is all too easy to become addicted to success and when the supply is stopped, the withdrawal symptoms are often acute; it can be a considerable blow when yesterday's idol realizes that he is today's nobody.

Financial security can provide a protective buffer against these difficulties, in that money in itself can be a lasting status symbol of the success which produced it. But such security can only be achieved by the professional sportsman, and not the true amateur, whose involvement in sport has almost certainly cost him time and money.

I was always aware that these matters would have to be faced some day and it may be because I often thought about my retirement that my present situation is a happy one with no regrets and few problems. I have been particularly fortunate in the career sense, because virtually the whole of my active sporting life coincided with my years as a student. I therefore began practising as an architect at exactly the same time as I would have done in the normal course of events, and my inter-national sports career could well prove only an advantage, if only from the public relations point of view. In this respect, I appear to disprove my earlier statements about the pitfalls of retirement, but it should be understood that I am one of a fortunate minority. The unlucky ones are the majority who leave school at fifteen and whose sporting careers therefore coincide with the crucial early years of employment. I could name half a dozen swimmers who at various times lost their jobs because of training and competition requirements. This situation is even more apparent in athletics, where an active international career usually begins later than in swimming. These amateur sportsmen find themselves as it were starting life again in their early or middle twenties with a great deal of ground to be made up in the business of earning a living, and very often they have only memories or a few plaques to show for their years in sport.

I have been fortunate also that the relative peace of my re-tirement is undisturbed by personality problems. Although I am no longer constantly in the limelight I find that I am not still plagued by a craving for attention and publicity, or to be more accurate, such needs which I have are being adequately filled. I think I have adjusted quite well in that respect, because throughout my career my father always tried to ensure that I kept my feet firmly on the ground and was not swept away by often heady Press notices. I think my stability in retirement (if the way of life of someone who until recently was a fun-loving twenty-six-year-old bachelor could ever be described as stable!) is also helped by the fact that I am now a professional swimmer, which means that I have retained a considerable link with my past life.

Being a professional does not mean that I now swim for money, but merely that I am paid for coaching. I also 'capitalize on my athletic fame', to use the official phrase, by writing newspaper articles, appearing in advertisements, and making personal appearances, and in general I now accept fees for my knowledge of swimming and for allowing the exploitation of the status which I achieved as a result of my successful career. But of course, I am now forbidden to take part in any swimming race or water-polo match held under the jurisdiction of any of the swimming associations.

Some amateur sportsmen find it difficult to become a professional but for many reasons this was not the case with me. I believe it is essential for the future well-being of British swimming that the professional coach be accepted totally by the amateur swimming associations and by the swimmers, as is the case in most other countries, particularly in the United States and Australia. This will necessitate a considerable change of attitude in both the governing bodies and the swimmers. The A.S.A. has already taken the first step in this direction by passing a motion last year that professionals be allowed to hold an official position within the organization, but British swimmers and clubs will also have to accept the hard fact that the best coaches must be paid. Swimming has come a long way since the days when an hour's training four or five days a week was considered more than adequate. Coaches nowadays must be prepared to spend upwards of three hours a day with their potential champions, and no one can expect that amount of time to be given without payment. It is the established practice abroad for club swimmers to pay their coach a flat rate of perhaps ten shillings per week, which covers all their coaching requirements. This is a very modest remuneration in relation to the time given, but the few pounds weekly which accrue to the coach in this way can make all the difference between his being able (coaches are usually *willing*) to give his time or not. Most swimming coaches throughout the world have other occupations and these comparatively small payments are necessary nowadays to offset the encroachments which coaching inevitably makes on the family life and the principal employment of coaches.

It was because I felt strongly about this that I have joined the growing band of professional coaches in Great Britain. My decision to become a professional was also given considerable impetus by the extent of 'shamateurism' which I experienced around the world. I met so many 'amateur' sportsmen, who were obviously making considerable capital out of their sporting prowess, that I decided to cash in when the opportunity presented itself. No amount of money would have tempted me while there existed even the remotest possibility of my winning an Olympic gold medal, but once that hope had gone, I had no hesitation in relinquishing my amateur status, and I actually corresponded with a well-known sports agency before I left Mexico City. This may well have been a violation of the Olympic Code, which states that no participant should even consider becoming a professional while the Games are in progress, but my competitive involvement was actually over, and whatever the interpretation of the rule, I feel satisfied that my years as a true amateur would be enough to outweigh this single indiscretion which I may have committed.

I said earlier that I had no regrets and this may appear somewhat improbable in the light of my four narrow defeats, which deprived me of four important titles, but I am being completely honest.

It is obviously a little frustrating to realize that a total of one solitary second of time, a few flicks of eyelid, meant the difference between my having one instead of five gold medals on the side-board, but the fortunes of international sport are governed by such minute fractions.

Out of seven years, which included some eighty to ninety major races, I lost only a handful, and although it would have been nice to have won them all, we must learn to come to terms with the disappointments of life, and sport is a great teacher in this respect. Very few men achieve all their ambitions and those who appear to do so often lose out in other respects. When I find myself wishing, as I sometimes do, that I had beaten Schollander in Tokyo, I always remind myself of the many thousands of swimmers all over the world who trained as hard as I and yet who did not even take part in an Olympic Games. I realize then how fortunate I have been and I get on with the job of trying to make my present and future life as satisfying as the past few years.

I am delighted to be still involved with the wonderful sport of swimming and I look forward to a long and happy association with what I believe will be a very different scene in the future. I foresee the barriers between the amateur and the professional disappearing altogether to make way for the kind of 'open' sport in which I would have greatly preferred to participate. Perhaps I will then regret that I was born too soon, as do so many former golfers, tennis players and footballers, who nowadays see the much improved career-potential of these sports. But in my case it would be a tiny regret in the flood of good fortune which swimming brought me.

Part 11

Learning to Swim
and
Training for Competition

Learning to Swim

There are three basic stages in learning to swim and they are as follows:

Stage 1
It is essential that the innate fear of water be overcome and replaced by a feeling of confidence.

Stage 2
After the feeling of confidence is developed, the learner must be taught how to place his body in the best possible position for executing the swimming skills.

Stage 3
After both confidence and correct body position have been established it is only a question of sustained practice. Under adequate instruction the learner will master the movements sufficiently well to feel safe in the water, and he will then derive the maximum pleasure from his newly-acquired ability.

It is the aim of this instructional chapter to show the simplest and most effective means of proficiency on all four swimming strokes: the breast-stroke, the back-stroke, the front-crawl and the butterfly.

It will help considerably if you are a member of a class which is receiving instruction, but if this is not possible try at least to have a companion, who is also a non-swimmer, so that you can watch and gain confidence from each other. And remember that practice makes perfect.

We have divided the course into fourteen lessons, and would

expect a pupil to spend at least thirty minutes on each lesson. Do not move to the next lesson until you are reasonably proficient at the previous one, even though this may mean spending several sessions in the water on the same exercise. Consolidate before moving on, and you will eventually become a better swimmer as a result of it.

LESSON 1
Gaining Confidence
This lesson is to familiarize the beginner with submerging the face, breath control and the realization of buoyancy.

1. Stand in chest-high water and submerge the face for ten seconds. Repeat for longer intervals with the eyes open when submerged, as it is of great value for the beginner to see that there are no hidden dangers underwater! There will be no discomfort or injury to the eyes in properly chlorinated swimming-pools.
2. The next step is to hold the rail at the edge of the pool and to practise 'bobbing'. Stand in water almost shoulder high. Take a normal breath and bend the legs until the top of the head is covered. Straighten the legs and breathe out again when your head is above water. Try it two or three times at first, then increase the number of 'bobs' till they can be done comfortably, as many times as you wish.
3. Gradually you should also practise breathing out while submerged. Try to time the whole movement so that you

begin to exhale as you begin the upward 'bob'. As the mouth breaks surface the exhalation should be completed, or nearly so, so that the short time above the surface is used mainly for the inhalation. Forcibly exhaling under water is the basis of the rhythmical breathing necessary in swimming most strokes.

LESSON 2

Gaining Confidence

Beginners must be made to realize very early that swimming is merely an extension of something that virtually everybody can do naturally, namely, floating. Our bodies are all naturally buoyant and the following exercises illustrate this facet. As the pupil is learning to swim on the front-crawl, I recommend that the buoyancy exercises should be carried out in the 'face down' position. If there is still a slight nervousness at keeping the face in the water, however, the first exercise may be done initially on the back before trying the face-down position. If necessary these exercises can be done at first with floatation aids.

1. Standing in shoulder-high water take a deep breath, bend your legs, lean forward with arms hanging loosely. Relax completely letting the water support you. In all floating exercises it is essential to take a good breath, as the air in one's lungs is a great aid to buoyancy.

2. In the same position, by grasping knees with your hands and pulling upwards towards your chest, the 'tuck' float

position can be attained. Do not panic if you immediately sink when first taking up the tuck position. This is quite normal, but the body will very soon bob up again.

3. From this position horizontal floating becomes possible by simply stretching out your body with your hands in front of you.

4. To stand from these positions simply press both hands downwards and back. This action brings the legs forward and into contact with the floor of the pool.

LESSON 3

Before being taught the complete front-crawl stroke, the beginner must be taught the elementary crawl known as the 'dog-paddle'.

Leg Action

The kick of the legs should be from the water surface downwards. It is simply a shallow paddling action, but without too much bend at the knees. The feet should pass one another almost vertically and opening from ten to sixteen inches. The whole of each leg plays its part and there must be no stiffness in the action which flows from the hip. The waist, trunk and shoulders are not allied to this movement and therefore should not be allowed to twist or sway.

This action can be practised in the following order:

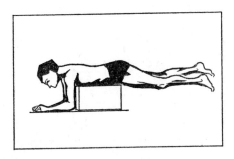

1. On dry land lying over a stool or bench.

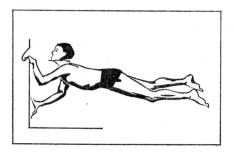

2. Holding on to the side of the pool with your body in the horizontal position.

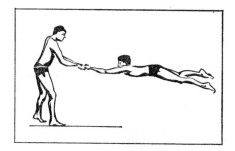

3. With a helper giving slight support to your arms and hands and pulling you slowly through the water.
4. Holding a floatation aid at arm's length and propelling yourself forward.

These leg actions should always be practised without undue muscular effort. Loose knees and ankles are essential.

LESSON 4

Arm Action of 'Dog-paddle'

Extend right arm forward about 4 ins below the surface. Commence pressure downwards with the right arm and immediately start a forward loose easy action of the left arm. When the left arm has reached an extended position the right arm should have been pulled slowly into a position below the shoulder, ready to be moved forward. A regular cycle of actions is then kept up by alternating the arm movements.

This action can be practised in the following order:

1. On dry land lying over a stool or bench.
2. Standing, bending slightly forward in water to shoulder height.

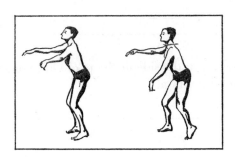

3. With a helper or floatation aid giving support to the waist.

Combine now the arm and leg actions. Initial movement can be introduced by pushing with the feet from the side or bottom of the pool. Practise the complete 'dog-paddle' stroke over extended distances. If further problems are found, watch any dog swimming and you will very clearly see why this technique is so named.

LESSON 5

When the pupil becomes reasonably confident on the 'dog-paddle' a beginning can be made with the standard front-crawl.

Arm Action

The arm action of the front-crawl can be divided into two movements:

1. The recovery (through the air).
2. The 'pull and push', which provides the propulsion.

1. *The Recovery*

The recovery is made loosely and quickly. The arm should be slightly bent and the elbow raised fairly well, with the

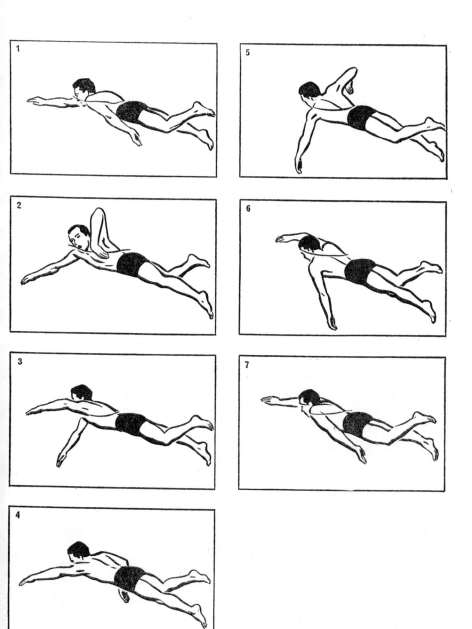

Lesson 5 – Front-crawl – surface view

M

hand and forearm completing a short semicircle. It is not a whole-shoulder movement but is made using freely the shoulder *joint*. The shoulder remains relatively still or flat until the recovery has been completed and the hand has entered the water.

2. *The 'Pull and Push'*

Once the hand has reached the water pressure is made slowly and deliberately. The pull and push is made with the arm slightly bent and the fingers closed. The hand should follow a line approximately along the centre line of the body. It is essential that the hand and forearm 'grip' the water, forcing it back and as a result propelling the body forward. These actions can be practised in the following order:

(1) On dry land lying over a stool or bench.

(2) Standing, bending slightly forward, in water to shoulder height.

(3) With a helper or floatation aid giving support to the waist.

The leg action of the front-crawl is similar to that of the 'dog-paddle', but as much more power is now coming from a longer arm pull, the leg action is shallower and straighter.

Before both movements can be combined satisfactorily, the breathing action must be practised.

LESSON 6

Front-crawl Breathing

When breathing is introduced into the front-crawl stroke the arm pull and recovery remain the same, and the head and neck movements facilitate air intake and output.

During every cycle of the arms the head is turned to one side sufficiently to bring the mouth above the water. This is done when one arm is fully extended forward and the other is ready for recovery. Breathing-in is done only with the mouth.

As the recovery arm moves forward for the entry of the hand, the head is returned to a downward and forward position where the breathing-out takes place. Breathing-out is done forcibly through both the mouth and nose. In this position the face is below the water, but not the forehead. The position is such that the slightest upwards tilt of the head will enable the eyes to look ahead.

The earlier 'bobbing' exercise should help with timing the above breathing action correctly.

The pupil is now ready to combine arm, leg and breathing actions of the front-crawl stroke.

LESSON 7

The complete front-crawl stroke co-ordinating the arm, leg and breathing actions takes a little practice.

At first move slowly forward on the legs while completing a few cycles on the arm action. To begin with, keep the head up and swivel to both sides to simplify breathing.

Gradually lower the head, breathing consistently to one side (whichever side feels natural). Breathe in time with every recovery of the arm on the breathing side.

The leg action should be relaxed. Six beats of the leg to every complete cycle of the arms. This 'six-beat crawl' is quite natural and does not have to be forced.

One should count '*one*, two, three, *four*, five, six'. It will help to begin with if you time the 'one' to the left hand entry and the 'four' to the right hand entry.

Always remember to grip the water with the hands which are very slightly cupped and the forearms, thus propelling yourself forward.

PRACTICE, PRACTICE, PRACTICE!!

It's easy!

LESSON 8

Once the beginner has mastered the 'dog-paddle' and the elementary crawl stroke the back-stroke is readily learned. Basically the back-stroke is an inverted crawl-stroke.

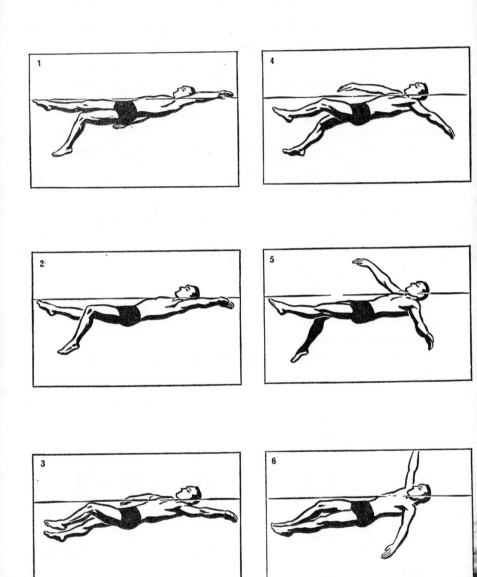

Lesson 8 – Back-stroke – side view

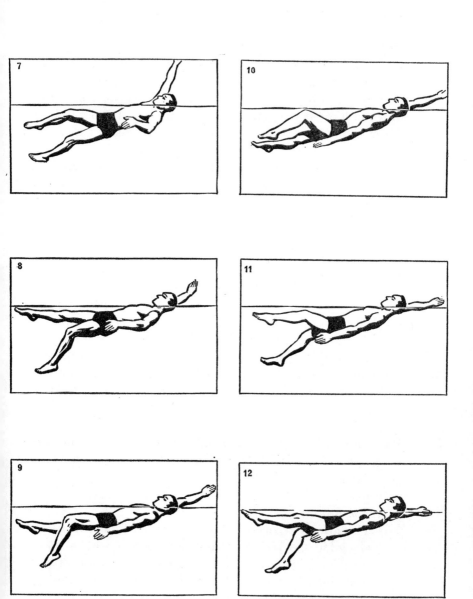

Lesson 8 – Back-stroke – side view (*continued*)

Body Position
Front-crawl position is inverted. The body should be relaxed but in as flat a plane as possible. The head should be held slightly up, with the eyes looking towards the knees. This action dips the hips very slightly and keeps the knees and feet in a lower position in the water to perform the leg-kick action.
Leg Action
Similar to front-crawl action. The depth of the kick should be between 12 in and 18 in. At the bottom of the kick the leg is bent at the knee and the instep of the foot points inwards and upwards. The foot being kicked upwards propels the body forward. Again, as in front-crawl, relaxation is important as is the flexibility of the joints.

The leg action should be practised with the help of a sculling action of the arms. To do this the arms and hands are kept underwater in a position alongside the hips. With the palms of the hands facing downwards the wrist and forearms are moved in a gentle circular action pressing the water downwards and the body upwards. An alternative method of practising back-crawl leg action is to hold a floatation aid across the chest and stomach and so retain the body in a suitable position for leg kicking.

LESSON 9
With very little practice you should now be quite at home on your back and should be experimenting with the back-stroke arm action.
Arm Action
  1. *Arm Recovery*
    The arm is recovered through the air from a position alongside the hip. It is a relaxed action with a loose shoulder movement. Do not throw any portion of the trunk into the action. The arm should be straight during the recovery and enters the water again well ahead of the shoulder – say about 1 o'clock, or 11 o'clock, if one imagines the head as being at the centre of a clock face. The arm action is, as in the front-crawl, an alternate

movement; while one arm is making the recovery through the air the other is making the 'pull and push' through the water.

2. *'Pull and Push'*

The arm enters the water behind the shoulders. The pull through the water is made by a sweep of the arm with the hand not more than 8–12 inches below the surface. This semicircular arm sweep is made away from the side of the head and shoulder with the arm slightly bent at the elbow. At waist level the wrist is flexed for the 'push' to the thigh. The hand is then lifted clear of the water and is ready for the recovery as the other arm is entering behind the shoulders for the 'pull and push'. Breathing offers no difficulty as both inhaling and exhaling are done above water level. A rhythmical breathing action is developed quite naturally.

As in front-crawl the complete stroke takes the form of six beats of the legs to every complete cycle of the arms.

LESSON 10

Breast-stroke should be attempted when the beginner has reached a reasonable speed and distance at crawl-stroke and back-stroke. Once again seek ease of performance from the start. It cannot be repeated too often that violent uncontrolled physical movement spoils good swimming.

Breast-stroke more than any other stroke needs perfect co-ordination to perform it well. It is not as attractive a stroke as the crawl and can only be attained by careful synchronization of both the arm and leg movements. It is not a natural stroke and some young children find the co-ordination necessary a bit too difficult.

Body Position

As in front-crawl it should be as flat as possible. The head is held quite high with the eyes looking forward. Apart from a slight bobbing movement the body should remain in a flat position throughout the stroke.

Unlike crawl and back-crawl most of the propulsion in breast-

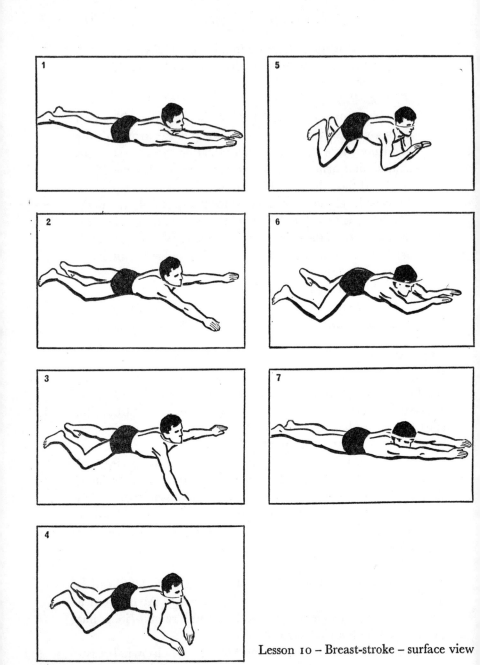

Lesson 10 – Breast-stroke – surface view

stroke comes from the legs and it is best to practice that part of the stroke first of all.

Leg Action

From the flat outstretched position the heels are drawn upwards towards the buttocks, the knees opening slightly at the same time. At the completion of this movement the heels are the width of the hips apart and the toes and knees are pointing sideways.

The heels are now swept in a semicircular action, sideways and outwards, then brought together again in a glide. It is this movement which provides the propulsion and should be developed into a strong vigorous action.

The leg action should be practised with a float held at arms length or by holding on to the rail at the side of the pool.

LESSON 11

Breast-stroke: Arm Action

Not much propulsion is supplied by the arms. The action keeps the head in a suitable position for breathing and the body in a position to achieve maximum benefit from the drive of the legs. From the flat outstretched position the hands are turned slightly outwards and pressed downwards and sideways till the arms are pulled back to shoulder level. The elbows are then bent and the hands brought together under the chin in a position ready to push forward to return to the stretched position. Unlike back-crawl and front-crawl both arms and both legs in breast-stroke perform the same movement at the same time, not alternately.

Breast-stroke: Complete Stroke

It is the arm action that starts the stroke. The leg action intervenes when the arms have been pulled to shoulder level. It is when the hands are drawn under the chin that the heels are drawn upwards towards the buttocks. Then the stretch forward by the arms and the push back and together by the legs are performed at the same time.

It is this *timing* that is difficult in breast-stroke. Always re-

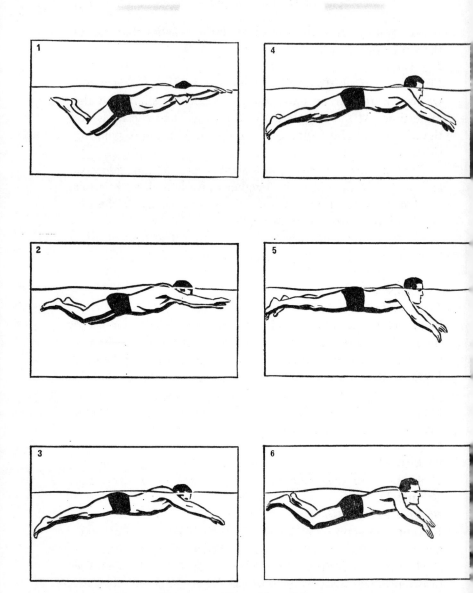

Lesson 12 – Butterfly – side view

Lesson 12 – Butterfly – side view (*continued*)

member that the legs do not move until the arms have been pulled to shoulder level.

Breast-stroke: Breathing

This comes naturally in breast-stroke. Inhaling takes place when the arm action puts the head at its highest position, i.e. when the arms are being pulled to shoulder level. Exhaling takes place as the arms are stretched forward. (Just remember – always *blow* your hands away.)

LESSON 12

The Butterfly Stroke (see previous page)

Many swimmers find the butterfly the most difficult stroke of all. This is not because the technique itself is complicated, but more because the action is physically very exhausting. We would therefore advise the adult beginner to attempt it only after a high degree of competence has been achieved on the other strokes. However, if the beginner is a child with the normal fitness and suppleness found in the young, we think this stroke can be taught as early as the front-crawl.

Leg-kick

The butterfly is often called the 'dolphin' or the 'fishtail', because the leg action is very similar to that of a fish. Once this leg movement is assimilated it is not normally too difficult to add the arm action and breathing.

Stage 1. Grip the scum channel or rail with both hands with the forearms against the wall and the elbows pointing to the bottom of the pool. Hold the body out flat near the surface and begin a gentle undulating motion by raising the hips and at the same time flicking downwards with the legs and feet. Keep the upper body as flat and steady as possible.

The legs are of course together throughout the action, although the feet are usually held in a 'pigeon-toed' position to increase the flexibility.

Stage 2. When a rhythmical movement has been achieved at the wall, the swimmer can then move to the next stage. Hold a small float in front of the body with the arms outstretched and after gently pushing off from the wall try to reproduce the above movement. Concentrate on raising the hips, not bending too much at the knees on the upward movement and particularly on the final 'flick' of the feet. The head can be held up for ease of breathing.

Stage 3. When the swimmer can comfortably and easily complete a width of the pool with the float, he can then repeat the action without it. The arms must be kept outstretched and together, the body flat with the face in the water, and the breath taken by lifting the head only (i.e. not the shoulders) after each second kick.

LESSON 13

Arm Action

Technically the arm action is very easy in that both arms do exactly the same movement at exactly the same time. It is extremely similar to the front-crawl action described in Lesson 5, except that the butterfly recovery is usually lower with straighter arms.

Stage 1. Stand in the shallow end with the water at shoulder level and both arms outstretched but slightly bent, in front of the shoulders. Press the hands down and push back to the thighs. Carry the arms round clear of the surface and back to the starting position. Repeat the action many times rhythmically, eventually pulling yourself across the pool, by walking on the bottom as you deliver the main power to the underwater action. Keep the head up for ease of breathing.

Stage 2. Place a float between the thighs and hold it firmly in place with the legs. Push off the wall or bottom and repeat the action of Stage 1 with the body flat on the surface and the face in the water. Breathe as the hands press down after each *second* arm entry. When breathing lift the head only (i.e. not the shoulders) and look to the front. As the hands press down immediately after entry, think of lifting the hips to the surface. Do nothing with the legs. Allow them to be quite relaxed apart from the pressure required to hold the float.

Stage 3. Discard the float and repeat the action of Stage 2 with the legs now completely relaxed. The hips should still be raised with each initial press of the hands and the breath taken in exactly the same manner as in the previous stage.

This is a difficult exercise, as the legs are giving no propulsion, but the arms are being strengthened and trained to dominate the action, as they do when the arms and legs are unified.

LESSON 14

The previous lesson should have given the swimmer a very good idea of the timing of the butterfly stroke, and it can now be profitably practised on the poolside before the final lesson begins.

Lean forward slightly and swing the arms in the normal butterfly manner. As the hands press down into the (imaginary) water flex the knees and say 'kick'. Repeat as the hands pass the hips.

Keep doing this until you have a bouncy, rhythmical action before moving into the water.

Once in the water think of the following main points:
1. Lie as flat as possible.
2. Keep the hips high.
3. 'Whip' downwards with the feet.

You will be very tired after practising this stroke, but the rewards in terms of improved physical condition and sense of achievement are well worth the effort.

Training for Competition

Throughout my book I have used the word 'dedication' many times to describe the correct attitude to training and competition. To many people it is a terrifying word, which suggests a monk-like existence devoid of any of the pleasures which most of us need to make life enjoyable. Everything is relative, however, and although I have known sportsmen who were dedicated in the most extreme sense, I myself never was, nor do I believe it necessary to cut oneself off from society in order to succeed at the highest level in sport. What is essential, however, is organization and it was because my time was meticulously organized, that I was able to carry on an almost normal student life throughout my competitive career.

There is undoubtedly something in the old saying that a busy man can usually find time for an additional task. A truly busy man could not get things done if he were not well organized, and the man who has mastered the art of organization can often achieve more than seems humanly possible. If we examine how we spend our time, most of us, even those who think we are busy, will find that we spend a considerable part of our time in a non-productive way. That part must be cut to a minimum when one is aiming for an ambitious target.

I was greatly helped in my endeavours by all the members of my family, who regularly submerged their own interests in a totally unselfish way, so that my training programme could function smoothly. I myself was dedicated in the sense that I stuck rigidly to the plan which we prepared in advance and I always worked very hard.

As you will see, my schedules allowed a considerable amount of time for enjoyment, which we considered essential to avoid the competitive staleness which would undoubtedly have followed if my life had consisted entirely of eating, sleeping, studying and training. I always allowed myself Tuesday, Friday and Saturday evenings off and as often as not, I spent them with my non-athletic friends in a normal student fashion. Even at the height of the competitive season I tried to have a break of a week or two for a relaxing holiday on the west coast of Scotland.

My schedules would have been considered only mildly demanding in comparison with those of the leading American competitors, but my nature would not lend itself to their kind of routine for more than a short period, and although several American coaches told me that I would have improved greatly under their system, I certainly would not have had as long a career as I did, nor would I have enjoyed swimming as much.

The detailed schedules which appear in the following pages are programmes copied directly from my log book and which I actually carried out. They are for a sprinter, of course, but the basic principles should be obvious, so that any distance swimmer could follow them merely by increasing the total training distance by between 50 and 100 per cent depending on the time at his disposal.

These programmes are for a one-season year, that is, aiming for one peak in the late summer. But if, as seems likely, British swimming moves into a two-season year, with peaks in March and August, then my programmes would naturally be 'concertinad' into two six-month cycles rather one of twelve months.

DIVISION OF THE YEAR

I divided my year into three basic stages as follows:

Period I – November till the beginning of February (October was 'wind-down' month from the previous season).

Period II – February till end of April.

Period III – May till end of competitive season (usually late September).

Each period could vary a little, of course, depending on the placing of the major competitive events, but once they were known and the plan had been decided upon, we tried to carry it out to the letter.

PERIOD I

Training Days: Sunday to Saturday

Sunday	1 swim session	1 weight session
Monday	1 swim session	1 running session
Tuesday	1 swim session	1 weight session
Wednesday	1 swim session	1 running session
Thursday	1 swim session	1 weight session

Friday – Free

Saturday – Free

SUNDAY

Weights 10 a.m. to 11 a.m.

1. Standing push-ups, 3 × 10 reps.
2. Standing push-backs from thighs, 3 × 10 reps.
3. Bench presses, 3 × 10 reps.
4. Bench pull-overs, 3 × 10 reps.
5. Squats, 3 × 10 reps.

Swim 11 a.m. to noon

500 yds warm-up, any stroke

4 × 400 yds arms only – 3-minute rest

2 × 400 yds individual medley – 5-minute rest   2,500 yds

MONDAY

Running 7.15 p.m. to 8 p.m. (town or cross-country)

Swim 8 p.m. to 9 p.m.

500 yds warm-up, any stroke

4 × 400 yds individual medley – 5-minute rest

5 × 100 yds butterfly with

100 yds freestyle legs between each rep.   3,000 yds

TUESDAY

Weights 7 p.m. to 8 p.m. Exercises as Sunday

Swim 8 p.m. to 9 p.m.

500 yds warm-up, any stroke

N

1,000 yds arms only, with legs tied with band
500 yds back-crawl warm-down   2,000 yds
WEDNESDAY
Running 7.15 p.m. to 8 p.m. As Monday
Swim 8 p.m. to 9 p.m.
   500 yds warm-up, any stroke
   4 × 200 yds medley – 2-minute rest
   4 × 200 yds arms only freestyle, with legs tied – 2-minute
   rest
   400 yds legs only warm-down   2,500 yds
THURSDAY
Weights 7 p.m. to 8 p.m. Exercises as Sunday
Swim 8 p.m. to 9 p.m.
   500 yds warm-up, any stroke
   4 × 400 yds arms only, with legs tied – 3-minute rest
   2 × 400 yds individual medley – 2-minute rest   2,900 yds
Notes

1. *Swimming* – None of the swimming was done to the point of fatigue. The aim was to finish each session tired but with something in reserve.

2. *Weight Training* – At the beginning the weights were selected so that no exercise could be done more than 12 times. They were increased throughout the period as strength increased so that each block of 3 × 10 repetitions always represented a near-maximum effort. I always began each weight session with five minutes of free exercises and five minutes skipping as a warm-up.

3. *General* – Throughout this entire period I engaged in several other activities which aided general body fitness. I played water-polo and football for the college team and often went for long walks. I always had a complete break of about a week at Christmas and New Year, when I enjoyed the festive season as much as anybody.

PERIOD 2 (February to end of April)
Training Days: Sunday to Friday

Sunday	1 swim session	1 weight session
Monday	2 swim sessions	1 pulley session[1]
Tuesday	2 swim sessions	1 weight session
Wednesday	2 swim sessions	1 pulley session
Thursday	2 swim sessions	1 weight session
Friday	1 swim session	

SUNDAY

Weights 10 a.m. to 11 a.m.

10 minutes general warm-up, skipping, jogging, etc.

Weights as left off from Period 1 with an increase in repetitions

Exercises – same, i.e.:

1. Standing push-ups 3 × 12 to 20 reps.
2. Standing push-backs from thighs 3 × 12 to 20 reps.
3. Bench press 3 × 12 to 20 reps.
4. Bench pull-over (straight arms) 3 × 10 to 20 reps.
5. Squats 3 × 10 to 20 reps.

Swim 11 a.m. to 12.30 p.m.

200 yds individual medley

500 yds free, slow

rest 10 minutes

Time trial – 25 yds or 50 yds or 75 yds or 150 yds

Rest 10 minutes or 300 yds kicking free

5 × 200 yds free with 4-minute rest

5 × 100 yds free

6 × 50 yds kicking

10 × 50 yds free with 1-minute rest

6 × 50 yds butterfly

300 yds arms only, with legs tied   3,500 yds

MONDAY

Morning, 7.30 a.m. to 8.30 a.m.

400 yds individual medley warm-up

500 yds arms only, with legs tied

200 yds back, arms only, with legs tied

[1] If no pulleys are available a few minutes of isometric exercises can be substituted.

2 × 400 yds freestyle – 5-minute rest
3 × 200 yds freestyle – 3-minute rest   2,500 yds
Evening
Pulley session
  Standing-pull, down and back, 3 × 30 reps.
Swim
  400 yds individual warm-up
  500 yds arms only, with legs tied
  200 yds back, arms only, with legs tied
  6 × 100 yds freestyle – 1-minute rest
  2 × 200 yds freestyle – 3-minute rest
  4 × 100 yds butterfly   2,500 yds
TUESDAY
Morning
  400 yds individual warm-up
  500 yds arms only, with legs tied
  200 yds back, arms only, with legs tied
  200 yds legs only
  10 × 100 yds arms only, with legs tied – 1-minute rest
  8 × 25 yds free – 15-second rest   2,500 yds
Evening
Weights 7 p.m. to 8 p.m.
Swim
  400 yds individual medley
  500 yds arms only, with legs tied
  200 yds back, arms only, with legs tied
  10 × 50 yds freestyle – 30-second rest
  200 yds legs only – rest
  10 × 50 yds freestyle – 30-second rest
  200 yds back-stroke   2,500 yds
WEDNESDAY
Morning
  400 yds individual medley warm-up
  500 yds arms only, with legs tied
  200 yds back, arms only
  8 × 75 yds freestyle – 1-minute rest

4 × 50 yds kicking – 10-second rest
6 × 75 yds butterfly – 1-minute rest   2,500 yds
Evening
Pulley session
  Pull down and back, 3 × 30 reps.
  1,000 yds freestyle swim
  10 × 50 yds freestyle – 30-second rest
  6 × 50 yds legs only – 10-second rest
  10 × 50 yds butterfly – 30-second rest
  200 yds back-stroke   2,500 yds
THURSDAY
Morning
  400 yds individual medley warm-up
  500 yds arms only, with legs tied
  200 yds back, arms only
  200 yds legs only
  3 × 400 yds freestyle   2,500 yds
Evening
Weights 7 p.m. to 8 p.m.
Swim 8 p.m. to 9.30 p.m. – Thursday Club Night: longer
  sessions
  400 yds individual medley warm-up
  500 yds arms only, with legs tied
  5 × 100 individual medley
  12 × 25 yds freestyle – 30-second rest
  6 × 50 yds freestyle – 45-second rest
  4 × 100 yds freestyle – 1-minute rest
  12 × 25 yds freestyle – 30-second rest
  100 yds warm-down   3,000 yds
FRIDAY
Morning sessions only
  500 yds easy swim
  200 yds legs only
  5 × 100 yds freestyle – 1-minute rest
  8 × 50 yds butterfly – 45-second rest
  8 × 50 yds freestyle – 1-minute rest   2,000 yds

Notes

1. *Swimming* – All the water work is now very hard and the emphasis is on the arms rather than the legs. We introduced time trials over a half, three-quarters and one and a half times the racing distance and these were done on a Sunday. For this reason the Friday session was usually slightly easier than the other days, and with the day off on Saturday a kind of 'taper' was completed before the time trial.

   There was usually some out-of-season competition available during this period and I would not normally alter my training unless it was a fairly important event (e.g. the British University championships) in which case a three- to four-day taper would be done. I would then aim to do a good time as an incentive to keep working hard.

2. *Weight Training* – The weights used at the end of Period 1 were not increased, but I increased the number of repetitions as high as would still permit me to do a maximum effort in three equal sets.

3. *General* – If possible try to train in a group, for competition in training is of great importance and is one of the main reasons for the success of the American swimmers.

   The really hard (and therefore beneficial) work has begun in this period, so try never to miss a session unless the reason is really important, e.g. examinations or illness. But do not 'kid' yourself into believing that you are ill, simply because the chlorine makes your eyes sore and your nose run. Remember that a quitter never wins and a winner never quits.

PERIOD 3
Training Days: Sunday to Friday

Sunday	1 swim session	1 weight session
Monday	2 swim sessions	1 pulley session
Tuesday	2 swim sessions	

Wednesday   2 swim sessions   1 pulley session
Thursday   2 swim sessions
Friday   1 swim session

SUNDAY

Weights 10 a.m. to 11 a.m. (Weights as left off from **Period 2**;
    no increase in repetitions)
Warm-up and time-trial as Period 2
Swim 11 a.m. to 12.30 p.m.

200 yds individual medley
500 yds arms only, with legs tied
100 yds legs only
200 yds back, arms only

} continuous

5 × 200 yds freestyle – 4-minute rest (4 × 50 yds with 20
    seconds)
5 × 100 yds freestyle – 2-minute rest (4 × 25 yds with 5
    seconds)

2,500 yds

MONDAY

Morning, 7.30 a.m. to 8.30 a.m.

200 yds individual medley
500 yds arms only, with legs tied
100 yds legs only
200 yds back, arms only

} continuous

10 × 100 yds freestyle – 1-minute rest (5 minutes after 6 reps.)
2 × 100 yds butterfly – 1-minute rest (4 × 25 yds with 5
    seconds)
3 × 100 yds freestyle – 1-minute rest (4 × 25 yds with 5
    seconds)

2,500 yds

Evening

Pulley session and skipping, 7.30 p.m. to 8 p.m.
Swim, 8 p.m. to 9 p.m.

200 yds individual medley
10 × 100 yds arms only – 30-second rest
6 × 50 yds legs only
4 × 100 yds freestyle – 2-minute rest

6 × 100 yds freestyle – 1-minute rest (4 × 25 yds with 5 seconds)

2,500 yds

TUESDAY

Morning, 7.30 a.m. to 8.30 p.m.

200 yds individual medley

500 yds arms only, with legs tied ⎫
100 yds legs only   ⎬ continuous
200 yds back, arms only   ⎭

5 × 200 yds freestyle – 3-minute rest

10 × 50 yds butterfly – 1-minute rest   2,500 yds

Evening, 8 p.m. to 9 p.m.

200 yds individual medley

5 × 200 yds freestyle – 4-minute rest (4 × 50 yds with 20 seconds)

3 × 100 yds freestyle – 2-minute rest (4 × 25 yds with 5 seconds)

2 × 200 yds freestyle – 2-minute rest

6 × 50 yds butterfly – 1-minute rest

12 × 25 yds freestyle with dive and turn – 30-second rest

2,500 yds

WEDNESDAY

Morning, 7.30 a.m. to 8.30 a.m.

200 yds individual medley

500 yds arms only, with legs tied ⎫
100 yds legs only   ⎬ continuous
200 yds back, arms only   ⎭

5 × 200 yds freestyle – 3-minute rest

6 × 75 yds freestyle – 1-minute rest

8 × 50 yds butterfly, arms only – 1-minute rest   2,500 yds

Evening, 8 p.m. to 9 p.m.

Pulley session and skipping

Swim

200 yds individual medley

5 × 200 yds freestyle – 4-minute rest (4 × 50 yds with 20 seconds)

5 × 100 yds butterfly – 2-minute rest
5 × 50 yds legs only – 10-second rest
5 × 100 yds butterfly – 2-minute rest
5 × 50 yds legs only – 10-second rest
12 × 25 yds freestyle, with dive and turn – 20-second rest

2,500 yds

THURSDAY

Morning, 7.30 a.m. to 8.30 a.m.

200 yds individual medley
500 yds arms only, with legs tied ⎤
100 yds legs only   ⎬ continuous
200 yds back, arms only   ⎦
5 × 100 yds freestyle – 1-minute rest
10 × 50 yds freestyle – 40-second rest
5 × 100 yds freestyle – 1-minute rest (4 × 25 yds with 5 seconds)   2,500 yds

Evening

200 yds individual medley
5 × 100 yds freestyle – 1-minute rest (4 × 25 yds with 5 seconds)
5 × 100 yds butterfly – 2-minute rest (4 × 25 yds with 5 seconds)
4 × 200 yds freestyle – 4-minute rest (4 × 50 yds with 20 seconds)
5 × 50 yds freestyle – 40-second rest
10 × 25 yds freestyle, with dive and turn – 20-second rest

2,500 yds

FRIDAY

7.30 a.m. to 8.30 p.m. (Distance session)

1,000 yds freestyle swim
2 × 400 yds individual medley
500 yds arms only
200 yds legs only   2,500 yds

Notes

1. *Swimming* – The basic aim of most of the water work done in this period is to train at the speed which one hopes to

achieve in competition. The racing distance was broken down into smaller distances with as short a rest as possible between the repetitions. As a sprinter I chose mainly 200 yds split into 4 × 50 yds with 20 seconds rest and 100 yds into 4 × 25 yds with 5 seconds rest. A distance man would work on 500's and 400's with longer rests. A dive was taken on the first repetition, but all subsequent ones were done with push-off. I used the 'tumble' turn in all training swims.

2. *Weight Training* – Some swimmers cease land work completely during the competitive season, but I always enjoyed my once-weekly session as it offered a change from the now almost exclusively water training.

3. *General* – As this period is one of really hard, high-quality work, it is essential that as much variety as possible is introduced into the schedule, if the ever-present danger of boredom is to be avoided. Provided that one never loses sight of the over-riding principle that most of the swimming must be done at competition speed, the work can be 'packaged' many different ways and the more variable the better the swimmer will like it.

THE TAPER

The extremely hard work which is now essential for first-class performances makes it absolutely necessary for the swimmer to have a recovery phase before a major effort. This period is extremely important, for the work of many months can be nullified, if the final few days are prepared imprudently. This preparation has been well named the 'taper', during which the broad base of work is tapered down in order to bring the swimmer to a well-rested peak.

It can take courage to cut down one's training drastically a week before a major event, but it is quite essential if an optimum effort is to be obtained in the race. My own taper lasted five to six days, during which I swam only once daily, doing a low number of repetitions of high-quality work with long rests between each effort. Each day I decreased the amount done on the previous day, but kept the quality very high. On the fifth day of the taper (or two days before the race) I always did a time trial over the full racing distance and on the day before the race I swam a relaxing 500 yds or did no swimming at all.

As a general rule it is better to do too little during the taper rather than too much, so *provided that you have worked very hard* in the weeks before your event, have the courage to do a proper taper and you will not regret it.

Sample training session during first day of taper:

400 yds warm-up
200 yds legs only
8 × 25 yds stroking (i.e. 90 per cent effort, but concentrating on technique) – 1-minute rest
8 × 50 yds – early repetitions slowish, building up to 100 per cent efforts on the last two or three – 3-minute rest
5 × 100 yds (each 4 × 25 yds with 5-second rest) – 4-minute rest between 100's
8 × 25 yds very fast, with dive – 2-minute rest
200 yds slow, wind down   2,100 yds

Sample schedule for fourth day of taper:

400 yds warm-up
8 × 25 yds stroking
4 × 50 yds – 3-minute rest
2 × 100 yds (i.e. 4 × 25 yds on 5 seconds) – 5-minute rest
2 × 25 yds with dive – 2-minute rest   1,200 yds

Other taper days are as above only varying slightly depending on how you feel and swim.

RACE DAY

I was always in bed by 10 p.m. on the evening before an important event. I normally read a little, then thought about my race in minute detail until I fell asleep. Sleep usually came very easily, but if it did not, I would relax my muscles from the toes upwards, consciously thinking of my ankles, calves, thighs, stomach, shoulders and neck. This always had me sound asleep within a few minutes.

I rose at 7 a.m. and had a shower or bath, then dressed in a leisurely fashion till I breakfasted at 8 a.m. on fruit juice, toast, honey, cereal and poached eggs.

Warm-up – My first warm-up swim was usually about 10 a.m. and consisted of the following:

Slow front-crawl till the arms were painful, then continuing until the soreness disappeared. In my case this usually entailed about 500 metres swimming.

200 metres easy backstroke

2 × 50 metres stroking

4 × 50 metres fast – 4-minute rest (third repetition to be fastest)

10-minute rest

Time trial over 100 metres at 95 per cent effort

(When my best times were just below 54 seconds, I aimed to do this time trial in 56 seconds or slightly better)

5-minute rest

4 × 25 metres fast

Dive – 2-minute rest

200 metres back-stroke, easy   1,400 yds

I would then go back to bed for a short time before lunch, which I always finished early enough to allow two hours to elapse before an afternoon race. If the event was in the evening I would again allow at least two hours after dinner. Both these meals would consist of fairly normal food, although I tried to choose easily-digestible items.

Final Warm-up – This usually took place 40 minutes before my race and followed the following pattern:

Shower (hot 5 minutes, cold 1 minute)

100 metres stroking (62–3 seconds)

2 × 25 metres fast, with dive

Turning practice in same lane as forthcoming race.

Hot shower (2 minutes) then cold shower ($\frac{1}{2}$ minute)

Rest and light massage till ten minutes before race

Rest until called by competitors' steward

I thought about the race constantly in the final few hours and always in a positive, confident manner. You are on your own when you stand on the block, so do not allow the slightest doubt to undermine your attitude. Every fibre of your body must be directed toward victory.